# News Flash!

Newspaper
Activities to
Meet Language-
Arts Standards
& Differentiate
Instruction

## by Danny Brassell

Crystal Springs
BOOKS

A division of SDE Staff Development for EDUCATORS

Peterborough, New Hampshire

Published by Crystal Springs Books
A division of Staff Development for Educators (SDE)
10 Sharon Road, PO Box 500
Peterborough, NH 03458
1-800-321-0401

www.crystalsprings.com
www.sde.com

Published 2007

Printed in the United States of America

11 10 09 08 07   1 2 3 4 5


ISBN: 978-1-884548-97-0

Library of Congress Cataloging-in-Publication Data


Brassell, Danny.

News flash! : newspaper activities to meet language-arts standards & differentiate instruction / by Danny Brassell.

p. cm.

Includes index.

ISBN 978-1-934026-12-0

1. Newspapers in education. 2. Language arts (Elementary) 3. Education, Elementary--Activity programs. I. Title.


LB1044.9.N4B73 2007

371.33--dc22


2007034233


Editor: Sharon Smith

Art Director, Designer, and Production Coordinator: Soosen Dunholter

This book is dedicated to all teachers willing to put scripted, mandated programs aside in their classrooms in order to introduce their students to authentic, engaging learning materials and activities. Thank you for remembering that learning and fun do not have to be mutually exclusive.

# Contents

# Acknowledgments

To me, the best part about writing books or articles is the opportunity to work with editors. I have never quite understood writers who have adversarial relationships with their editors, as editors are paid to make writers' writing look better. I have been blessed to work with a lot of great editors, and Sharon Smith has been a delight to have as an editor at Crystal Springs for this project. Her feedback has been thorough, timely, and positive, and I greatly appreciate all of her efforts.

This book would not exist without the support of Lorraine Walker. I pitched her a list of 20 ideas, and I had a pretty good idea which ones would intrigue her. I want to thank Lorraine for allowing me to write this book rather than the one on differentiated assessments.

I must mention my profound thanks to Soosen Dunholter for a book design that blew me away. It is a rarity to encounter a book in education that is teacher friendly and visually appealing, but Soosen managed to make this both.

The Newspapers in Education (NIE) program has constantly inspired me with its ideas for exposing students to the benefits of newspapers. While each newspaper runs its own NIE program independently, nieonline.com provides an online "warehouse" of ideas and teaching tips on its Web site (http://nieonline. com), as well as weekly lessons categorized by grade level via Hollister Kids (http://www. hollisterkids.com). NIE has developed many excellent materials that served as the catalyst for this text, including a list of 100 ways to use the newspaper (many developed by Dr. Darla Shaw and supplemented by Wendy Grimshaw). I am indebted to the Newspaper Association of America and Online Publications Inc. for their support of NIE. If we had more people in education like those affiliated with NIE, I am convinced we would have no problem motivating students to read and write.

My gorgeous wife, Jeanie, and my beautiful children, Kate and Sean, put up with Daddy constantly getting up at 4 A.M. and often coming home around 10 P.M. Between writing and speaking, I spend too much time away from family. I thank them for reminding me from time to time that walks on the beach, Saturday matinees, and weekly church visits are just as important as the work I too often allow to overwhelm my thoughts. The three of them are essential to my high spirits.

Finally, I became a teacher only after I was a journalist. Both careers proved to be rewarding and educational experiences, and my struggles in the classroom allowed me to better appreciate how important inspirational teachers can be. I want to thank all of my journalism professors at American University who encouraged me to write: Steve Taylor, Wendy Williams, Richard Stout, Rodger Streitmatter, Dom Bonafede, and Rose Ann Robertson. I'd also like to thank Bette Dickerson, who encouraged me to add sociology as a major and teach in the inner city. All of these individuals exemplify how good teachers make a difference, and they showed me that the best teachers tend to "push the envelope" by extending learning beyond textbooks.

# Introduction

I hate textbooks. They give me the creeps and put me to sleep. Think back to when you were a child. Can you recall your favorite textbook? If nostalgic thoughts of nights spent cuddling with your mother under an afghan and reciting exercises from your third-grade math book just popped into your head, you probably do not need to read this book. The textbooks your school provides probably satisfy your hunger for learning materials.

However, my elementary school students despised textbooks, as have thousands of others I have observed in other classrooms. Most of the textbooks I see for elementary school students are drier than the finger-paint stains on a student's sweatshirt, and many textbooks provide little in the way of meaningful instruction. What is a teacher to do?

If you're a typical classroom teacher, you want learning materials that you can use tomorrow. With a little luck, the lessons and activities are research based and cover content standards. With lots of luck, students enjoy the lessons and activities. I know you do not have time to compare this theory with that or to extensively research what resources are needed to successfully complete a particular unit. You do not need a resource that is suited only for a specific standardized program (since standardized programs are likely to change more frequently than a student's excuses for being late to class). You need a resource you can count on whenever you teach and wherever you go.

Newspapers are the answer.

## Why Am I Such an Advocate for Newspapers in the Classroom?

I love newspapers.

My entry into the American workforce began with newspapers. When I was only eleven years old, I worked in the circulation department of the *Waterloo Courier* in Waterloo, Iowa.

More specifically, I was a paperboy. I had sixty-two houses on my route and could cover loading and delivering all of the newspapers in my bag in just under two hours, provided the Richters' beagle did not bite my ankle and Mr. Shaw did not share one of his stories from his days as an assistant supply officer in the South Pacific during World War II.

To say that I was interested in newspapers would be a gross overstatement. I despised newspapers, especially the Sunday edition. Sundays meant getting up before dawn reared its nasty head and carrying newspapers that were more than three times the size of a typical weekday edition. The only thing I thought the newspaper was good for was an income that could sustain my thirst for chocolate milk shakes at the Hardee's fast-food restaurant near the end of my route.

In time, though, I decided that newspapers were not all that bad. I believe I decided that when I saw my name in the newspaper for the first time. An ego was born.

Press the fast-forward button to my college years in Washington, D.C. There I discovered that not only did I enjoy reading newspapers, but I enjoyed writing for them as well. I majored in print journalism and loved covering important events such as presidential campaign rallies and museum exhibit openings. I cherished moments when editors assigned me stories that afforded me the chance to learn about diverse topics, from the causes and effects of carpal tunnel syndrome to the history of the Main Reading Room at the Library of Congress.

As a senior, I worked for a newspaper that put me in contact with all of the major (and most of the minor) newspaper editors in the country. I had several offers to choose from after graduation, and the editor of one of the oldest and most prestigious newspapers in the United States offered me a coveted job as a city beat reporter. The only catch was that I would start out earning a salary of a little under $17,000 a year. I believe I could have earned more if I had applied for welfare.

**B**roke, I had no trouble choosing to become a teacher for the noblest of reasons: it paid better than newspapers. As pathetic as it may sound, I chose to become a teacher for the high pay.

I explored other options, and I stumbled upon a teaching position in inner-city Los Angeles that offered $25,000 a year. Broke, I had no trouble choosing to become a teacher for the noblest of reasons: it paid better than newspapers. As pathetic as it may sound, I chose to become a teacher for the high pay.

While I dreamed of becoming the teacher in the movies who inspires his high school students to go to college, a series of grade-level changes found me becoming an early elementary-school teacher. Instead of preparing my students to ace AP exams, I returned from a long day at work with marker stains and dried glue around my kneecaps, the remnants of hugs showered upon me throughout the school day by my little ones. My students were less concerned with which college to choose than with tattling on one another.

Teaching in under-resourced areas with few or no books of any kind (even textbooks), I turned to the resources that I knew were cheap, interesting, and constantly updated: newspapers. It did not matter that we did not have textbooks; daily newspapers provided all of the necessary elements to teach objectives in every content area. Since newspapers offer something for everybody, they also appealed to the interests of all of my students. As much as I loved newspapers before, I considered them to be a blessing from a higher deity when I was searching for resources that could teach and inspire students at the same time.

A newspaper is an inexpensive, renewable resource that is the equivalent of having a brand-new textbook each and every day. Newspapers offer every student something of interest, whether it be a funny comic strip or last night's basketball scores, movie times or directions for buying tickets to a Wiggles concert. This book provides practical mini-lessons to use with newspapers. The activities are easy to implement and address the content standards that are common to many states. Textbooks may cover those standards, but they often fail to capture students' interest. This book shows how flexible and adaptable newspapers can be in teaching English/language-arts objectives. I believe that, used properly, a daily newspaper can be a richer, more useful resource than any textbook.

## How to Use This Book

A good news story is organized like an inverted pyramid. The most important information comes first. The "lead," or opening, sentences of a news story should answer the questions who, what, when, where, why, and how—known collectively as the five Ws and an H. The first chapter of this book attempts to answer all of those questions as it examines the rationale behind using newspapers to teach your students, offers advice on the best times during the school day to use newspapers, and suggests ways to obtain copies of newspapers for all of the students in your class. The second chapter provides mini-lessons that introduce students to newspapers.

The remaining chapters represent the nuts and bolts of this book: mini-lessons designed to teach and reinforce a wide range of specific English/language-arts objectives. The mini-lessons cover the four essential aspects of language development: listening, speaking, reading, and writing. Each mini-lesson contains a lesson plan for teachers. Where appropriate, reproducible pages also are included to help guide students through the activities. However, not every activity requires students to write (on a reproducible or otherwise). In some cases, discussion will do just fine.

## This Book Is a Starting Point

I have provided fifty-seven cool lesson plans, many with reproducibles, for students in grades 1–3. Do not feel as if you have to use these lessons exactly as I have written them. You will not hurt my feelings by "liberating" one of my ideas (thieves steal; teachers liberate) and turning it into something more appropriate for your students. Please feel free to adapt these lessons for other purposes, too. Although this book provides ways to use newspapers specifically for teaching English/language arts, I hope you will also use it as a springboard for creating newspaper-based activities for your broader curriculum.

Besides complete lesson plans, I have included a number of "extra" ideas. I wanted this book to read like a newspaper, and not all of the best ideas in newspapers come from detailed stories. Sometimes all a reader needs is a chart, an announcement, or an advertisement to spur her interest. For teachers who prefer ideas over detailed lesson plans, I have inserted additional teaching suggestions, extension activities, and thoughts on how to differentiate instruction for all students.

Every student in your class is different, and this book strives to address the needs of all of your students, not just the few who will benefit from any enhancement exercise you present. Differentiation—whether it refers to curriculum, instruction, or assessment—does not mean teaching different students different things. When I talk about differentiating, I mean teaching the same concept in different ways, based on the interests and skills of individual students. Every class I have ever taught has included a broad range of learning styles and abilities, and this book offers lots of ideas for differentiating your instruction in ways that tap into each student's strengths.

Nowadays, teachers face a lot of competition for students' attention. My goal is that by the time you finish this book, you will have all kinds of ideas for using newspapers in your classroom every day. If you can draw students into the habit of reading a newspaper each day (even if it is just the sports page or comics), I believe there is a good chance you can encourage them to become interested in reading. The more interested students become in reading, the more likely it is that they will read. And the more they read, the better they will be at it.

## A Final Note

The most important people I know teach first, second, and third graders. These are the teachers who help young children decide whether they enjoy school or dread it. As an early-elementary-school teacher, you can make a huge difference in your students' lives every day. I hope you find this book helpful. Good luck, and enjoy every moment you spend teaching English/language arts with newspapers.

# Why Use Newspapers—

CHAPTER
1

## and Where to Get Them

What's black and white and read (pronounced *red*) all over? The newspaper! Get it?

Well, maybe you're not rolling down the aisle laughing, but my second graders howled for minutes after hearing that riddle. Of course, they then spent the next half hour rattling off to me every horrible joke or nonsensical anecdote they had ever heard. No matter; I always breathed a sigh of relief whenever I could get my students excited about anything during my first year of teaching. I owe much of my remaining sanity (and there is not much left) to newspapers.

Newspapers offered me one of my first successes as an elementary-school teacher. When I began teaching, I put on a good show with my enthusiasm, but I had practically no clue about what I was doing. Whoever thinks teaching is easy needs to spend a month in a classroom. There is nothing tougher, and I have the gray hairs and nervous jitters to prove it. I have often heard the comment that if you can make a difference in the life of at least one of your students, you have truly succeeded. But I say that if you make a difference in the life of only one of your students, you are a colossal failure and should go back to plucking chickens or selling stocks or whatever it was that you used to do. Heck, I can *accidentally* make a difference in the lives of three or four students. We need teachers who make a difference in the lives of *most* of their students.

If there is one thing I have learned as an educator, it is that passion is contagious. Teachers need to teach what they know and love. I can tell you what a teacher's interests are just by looking at her students. If Mrs. Hamilton's students enjoy performing science experiments, my guess is that Mrs. Hamilton likes science. When I see Ms. Barter's students performing skits and recitals all the time, something tells me that Ms. Barter has an attraction to performing.

I like newspapers.

Newspapers are great. Whether you teach in a metropolitan, suburban, or rural area, you have access to newspapers. Some are daily, and others are weekly. Some are free at corner newsstands, and others will set you back a couple of quarters. Newspapers are useful, as they provide information that is critical to everyone, from crime statistics to department store ads to the cost of a used Chevy pickup. The uses of a newspaper are endless, and I was always fascinated to hear students tell me about their favorite sections of the newspaper.

If you had asked me what part of the newspaper the typical second grader would turn to first, I would have guessed the comics or sports page. My students, however, immediately turned to the weather map, as they were eager to show me some new state, city, or country they had learned about. I am a huge fan of teaching geography, as it seems to me that the only way most Americans learn about geography is through wars or natural disasters. Just about every American kid can point out Iraq or New Orleans, but many students cannot point out where they live. My students wanted to impress me with their newfound geographical knowledge because geography matters to me. Again, students' interests have a way of reflecting their teacher's, and it became apparent that my students loved looking at weather maps and working with newspapers because those things are important to me.

What I treasure most about newspapers is that they deal with the here and now. They are meaningful. Many textbooks deal with subjects that are so foreign to young students that they might as well be explained in another language. Newspapers are written in a concise fashion that gets to the point, and they deal with a wide array of current events. If I ask a first grader to guess what the weather is going to be for the rest of the week, that may prompt her to check out the weather forecast. Asking "Does anybody know how many points LeBron James scored last night?" may inspire a group of third graders to scour the sports page.

As students work with maps, they see how useful newspapers will be throughout their lives. Newspapers are constantly updated resources, providing motivation for reading and discussion. They can be cut, marked, clipped, pasted, filed, and recycled—and no one will flip out. Essentially, newspapers bridge the gap between the classroom and the "real" world. Walk into a coffee shop or library or office, and you'll be much more likely to see people reading newspapers than to see them reading textbooks.

This book provides you with real-world tools you can use daily to the benefit and delight of your students. In my classes, usually one of my students distributed newspapers to his classmates at the very beginning of class, and just about everyone read on her own, with a buddy, or in a small group while I read my newspaper aloud to a couple of struggling readers. (They were usually boys, and we usually read a sports article.)

My students loved beginning their day with ten or fifteen minutes of newspaper reading, as it prepared them for the morning meeting. The keen student observers knew that they'd benefit from noting the date, the weather forecast, the birthdays of famous people, and other tidbits that we reviewed during our morning meeting. They also knew that I'd reward anyone who could find all of the words in our "thought for the day" in the newspaper's headlines. Each student knew he was to cut out the words and paste them on a card to give to me. Those who found all of the words would get bookmarks, journals, loans of "special" books (those autographed by authors, expensive pop-up books, or books from my private collection), or other reading privileges.

Speaking of cutting and pasting, this might be a good time to note that newspapers can often be messy. I am one of those neat freaks who appreciates a tidy classroom as much as the next teacher, but you need to focus on creating an environment that gets kids excited to be in school. Messy rooms can always be cleaned up; boring rooms require more complex solutions. One of my cherished goals was to see students

## Train the Parents

Mark Twain once wrote that when he was eighteen, his father did not know anything, and when he was twenty-one, he could not believe how much his father had learned in the past three years. Being a parent is one of the most important roles a person can play, and most of us are completely unprepared for the job. As teachers, we need to help parents understand how they can help us help their children.

If you are going to send newspapers home with your students, why not offer a couple of workshops for parents to show them how they can reinforce English/language-arts skills with newspapers at home? I used to provide training sessions for my students' parents every other Friday after school in my classroom, and the parents constantly thanked me. I never showed them anything that required a lot of time or a doctorate in education. I just taught them how they could work on some simple behaviors with their children.

Yes, it took a little extra time to facilitate these meetings. But it never ceased to amaze me how much more smoothly my class ran once I had parents reinforcing my lessons at home. If you get the parents on your team, you can move mountains.

from other classes looking through our classroom windows in awe, wishing they could join us.

I allowed my students to work with newspapers throughout the classroom. I could find students at the writer's workshop center drafting stories to submit to the classroom newspaper we published for parents and the community. I could find other students in our classroom library relaxing on cushions and reading articles to stuffed animals. Still other students would be clipping adjectives from newspapers so they could construct poems for our poetry coffeehouse night.

Use newspapers wherever, whenever, and however you can. Your students will love you for it, and you will enjoy teaching more.

## Teaching English/ Language-Arts Objectives with Newspapers

I am not what you would call a big phonics guy. Some teachers cannot get through the day without leading their students in a chorus of "Aaa-aaa-al-li-ga-tor! Bbb-bbb-ball! Kkk-kkk-cat!" I could walk into most classrooms across America at 9:40 A.M. and see teachers leading their classes in animal gestures and noises that sound like the cries of wounded creatures.

People with lots of degrees after their names claim that most teachers teach the way they learned. My own experience supports that, as phonics was not the way I learned to read. I come from a home in which my parents always read in front of me and to me, and I cannot remember a day when I did not see both of them reading books, magazines, pieces of mail, or the newspaper. My home was a print-rich environment, and I don't recall my parents ever saying, "Danny, would you like a b-b-b-book?"

That's not to say phonics does not have a place in a teacher's curriculum. I know that I did not benefit from explicit phonics instruction when I was a child, but that does not mean it doesn't work. Teachers who have been around for a while are wise enough to recognize that every student learns differently. The prestigious

educator Howard Gardner refers to this as students exhibiting "multiple intelligences." A popular saying puts it another way: "different strokes for different folks." Many students benefit from phonics instruction, so I taught phonics. Teachers must adapt to their students' needs—not the other way around.

That is where newspapers come to the rescue.

Daily newspapers offer a daily lesson in phonemic awareness, decoding, and word recognition. They are excellent tools for enhancing students' vocabulary development and assessing reading comprehension. Because newspapers include many forms of writing—from stating the facts in a news story to persuading people to purchase products in advertisements—they inspire students to write in different ways. Since there is something of interest for everybody, newspapers also provide great material to use in practicing speaking and listening skills.

Heck, if you give me one daily newspaper from any state, I bet I can cover every single English/language-arts objective within that state's standards framework with that newspaper. And I can do it all while keeping in mind the advice of a great philosopher: Mary Poppins. She said, "For every job that must be done, there is an element of fun." To me, that translates into one thing: games are good. Newspapers are an excellent resource for teaching students fun games they can play on their own. Students don't necessarily need to know that these "games" help reinforce their understanding of the relationships between sounds and print. By turning any of my newspaper mini-lessons into a game, you can encourage students to read newspapers on their own—and in the process reinforce their understanding of many literacy concepts.

## Differentiating Instruction with Newspapers

Well-educated folks at prestigious universities love to throw around fancy education terminology. Whether you want to consider students' "multiple intelligences" or facilitate a "differentiated classroom" is up to you. The important thing to remember is that each student has unique needs. Your job as an educator is to make your instruction accommodate the specific needs of each student. Newspapers make this easy, as they meet the needs of all learning modalities.

A word of advice: don't try to do it all yourself. You will discover that you have students in your classroom who are eager to provide leadership and guidance to their classmates. Let them! The more control you hand over to your students, the more you allow their individual strengths to shine. For example, I enjoy writing songs, but I always allowed students to write songs that taught specific objectives. Some of my students insisted on leading certain lessons, and

I always allowed them to do so (as long as they had shown that they could handle it).

Students can help in another way, too. I used to complain about how difficult it was to figure out different ways for students to demonstrate that they understood something. My mistake was that I was trying to think of how to accommodate each student entirely on my own. But most of my best ideas were the direct results of conversations with individuals under four feet tall (my first, second, and third graders, that is). I also allowed students in small groups to think of different ways they could demonstrate that they understood something. (They could sing, draw, act, graph, etc.) Choice is a key part of differentiation and a great motivator.

# Howard Gardner's Eight Ways of Being Smart

**1 Verbal/Linguistic:** This student is strong in reading, writing, speaking, and listening. She likes reading books and being read aloud to. She tells jokes and anecdotes to classmates and enjoys writing stories.

**2 Logical/Mathematical:** This student is strong in math, reasoning, logic, problem-solving, and noticing patterns. She enjoys solving riddles, is curious about how things work, and calculates math problems easily.

**3 Visual/Spatial:** This student is strong in reading maps and charts, drawing, visualizing, and imagining things. She enjoys coloring pictures, creating interesting designs, watching movies, and reading charts and maps.

**4 Bodily/Kinesthetic:** This student is strong in athletics, dancing, acting, handicrafts, and using tools. She enjoys moving around, working with her hands, and practicing activities rather than listening to explanations of how they work.

**5 Musical/Rhythmic:** This student is strong in picking up sounds, singing, and remembering melodies and rhythms. She enjoys listening to music and playing instruments, and she works better when music is playing.

**6 Interpersonal:** This student is strong in understanding people, leading, organizing, communicating, resolving conflicts, and selling. She enjoys being the center of attention, working with others, and talking.

**7 Intrapersonal:** This student is strong in understanding herself, recognizing strengths and weaknesses, and setting goals. She enjoys working alone, reflecting, and pursuing her interests.

**8 Naturalist:** This student is strong in understanding nature, sorting, and classifying. She enjoys spending time outdoors, sees details in nature, and classifies things into categories.

Keep in mind that everyone exhibits characteristics of one or more intelligences.

## Obtaining Newspapers for Your Classroom

I used to walk a different student home from school every day. I could do that because my school served the surrounding neighborhood. Although I knew my students came from under-resourced home environments, I did not fully understand what that meant until the day I walked Hector Hernandez home. (I have changed all student names for privacy reasons.) His mother graciously invited me into their three-bedroom home, which they shared with three other families. There was only one lightbulb in the house, and Hector shared a bed with his mother, father, and baby sister. Beside that bed were the only reading materials I found in the entire house: the newspapers I had sent home with Hector.

In many years of teaching, I have learned that I cannot control students' home environments. Not all students come to school with the same resources. Some come hungry, and others come worried about immigration officers raiding their homes and deporting their families. The one thing I could provide every one of my students was a copy of the newspaper.

While your students' home situations may not be so dire, getting newspapers for your class should be a top priority. How can you do that? Newspapers in Education (NIE;www.nieonline. com) is one of my favorite resources for teachers. Serving more than 3 million students of 90,000 teachers in more than 16,000 schools, the NIE program provides teachers with copies of local newspapers for all of their students at least once a week. (The NIE Web site is also a wonderful source of lesson plans across curricular areas for students of all ages.) Many major dailies across the country participate in NIE, and sometimes local businesses help to fund the program so that the papers are available for free to under-resourced schools. To see if you can take advantage of this program to get free or discounted newspapers for your students, call your local newspaper and ask for the education representative in charge of Newspapers in Education. Teaching in Los Angeles, all I had to do was call the education representative of any area newspaper and ask for free newspapers for my students.

If you teach in a more affluent area, NIE may not provide free newspapers for your students. However, you still can participate in NIE programs that will supply your students with thousands of newspapers at a minimal cost to your school. (Tip: I have found that many businesses will help offset the cost, especially if you and your students write thank-you notes and

# Carol Ann Tomlinson's Four Characteristics of a Differentiated Classroom

**1** **Instruction is concept focused and principle driven.** Students all explore and apply the same key concepts, and they have the opportunity to display their understandings in different ways.

**2** **Differentiation builds in ongoing assessment** of students' readiness as well as growth. The teacher continually assesses her students' needs so she can adapt instruction accordingly.

**3** **The teacher implements flexible grouping for her students.** Students are given opportunities to work individually, with partners, and in small groups. Grouping is arranged according to students' needs and varies throughout the day. Groups sometimes include mixed abilities.

**4** **Differentiated classrooms allow students to be active, independent learners.** Teachers act as facilitators, empowering students to learn on their own.

invite businesspeople to come see your classroom activities for themselves.)

Another alternative is to ask students to bring in day-old newspapers from home. Yesterday's news works perfectly well for most of these English/language-arts activities, and most parents will be happy to send their recycling in your direction.

If you do not teach in an urban area with one or more major daily newspapers, but your community has a smaller weekly newspaper, everything in this book can be adapted to meet your needs. Although smaller weekly newspapers do not provide as much printed material as the larger dailies and thus may require teachers to conserve a bit, they are wonderful resources. In fact, friends of mine who have taught in rural areas have said how much they enjoyed working with their local newspapers, because their students developed close relationships with newspaper employees—and their affection for newspapers grew exponentially.

One suggestion for teachers in smaller communities is to supplement weekly newspapers with articles downloaded from the Web sites of major dailies. Most major daily newspapers offer free Internet editions. (See the list of Web sites on page 137.)

## Show Off

Be proud of your students! Show off their skills to parents, the school, and the community. If your local newspaper is gracious enough to supply your students with free newspapers for a semester, invite people who work for the newspaper to your classroom. Create a program that shows your guests all of the skills your students have learned from reading the newspaper. Who knows, your class may even be featured in a story published in the newspaper.

Teaching in a metropolitan area serving students in an under-resourced school, I managed to secure a different free newspaper for each of my students every day of the week. Every day I stopped by the main office, grabbed my stack of thirty-three newspapers, and happily delivered it to my classroom. Robin Hood probably never felt this good.

# Getting to Know Newspapers

**CHAPTER 2**

These days, information overwhelms us. Like every "old-timer," I like to tell children how hard I had it and how easy they have it. I'm not sure that is really the case, though. Imagine being seven years old and trying to navigate the world of textbooks, cable television, Internet blogs, cell phone text messages, satellite radio, iPods, and newspapers, to name just a few forms of communication. Kids nowadays deal with E-mail, snail mail, blackmail—it has become ridiculous. I would not be surprised to see Americans evolve a third eyeball, as children need to learn from a young age how to multitask and decipher information quickly.

Once, my principal reprimanded me for allowing my students to cheat on an exam. I did not exactly allow my second graders to cheat. You see, if they paid attention, they would notice that all of the answers to the exam questions were posted on bulletin boards and pocket charts throughout the classroom. Many students figured that out and scored very well. I explained to the principal that in today's world it was more important for students to understand how to access information than simply to memorize random facts. She wrote me up anyway, but I still think I was right.

With so many sources of information available, it is important that students learn how to find the information they need. Working with newspapers on a daily basis can help them learn how to gather, analyze, and use information in ways that will benefit them as they work with all forms of media.

One caveat: before you use newspapers in your classroom, it is a good idea to discuss the matter with your students' parents, your principal, and the newspaper(s). Sometimes newspapers contain material that may not be suitable for first, second, or third graders. A couple of examples that come to mind are photos of car accidents and advertisements for women's lingerie. Although I am convinced that most children see thousands of negative and inappropriate images before they ever step into a classroom, you do not want to be the object of a parent group's picketing campaign. Sneak a peek at the newspaper each day before you distribute it to your students. If you find any questionable material, you can ask one of the fifth-grade teachers at your school to send over a couple of her best-behaved students to remove the material from the newspapers for your class.

As part of most states' English/language-arts standards for grades 1–3, students need to be able to read and understand grade-level-appropriate material and be familiar with specific concepts about print. Most states expect that, in addition to their regular school reading, students will read half a million words annually from a variety of grade-level-appropriate narrative and expository texts. Besides textbooks and high-interest books found in your class and school libraries, you need to expose students to other forms of text—the kinds of material found in magazines, on the Internet, and in newspapers. The following mini-lessons are meant to provide an introduction to newspapers—to expose students to newspapers' various structural features and reinforce basic concepts about print.

# Listen Up!

**H**ere is your chance to get your students pumped up about using newspapers and at the same time get them up and moving around the classroom. I urge you to promote all of the content found in newspapers, from stories and comics to coupons and weather maps. I liked to brag about my favorite sections before asking students to share their favorite items. In this way, the activity can double as a "show and share" interactive activity, which students tend to treasure.

You can differentiate this activity by allowing students to take on specific roles. For example, some students can act as spokespersons for their groups, others can be in charge of organizing students according to their interests, and some can even "perform" their favorite sections of the newspaper in skits and songs.

## WHAT YOU NEED

### FOR EACH STUDENT

- **reproducible**
- **newspaper**
- **pencil**
- **yellow crayon**

### FOR THE TEACHER

- **marker**
- **6 index cards**

## OBJECTIVE

Students will listen attentively.

## PROCEDURE

1. Before class, make sure the categories listed on the reproducible are appropriate for the newspaper you're using. Make any necessary adjustments, then make copies of the reproducible.
2. Write each category listed on the reproducible on a separate index card.
3. Place the cards in different areas of the classroom.
4. In class, hand out all of the materials.
5. Give students a chance to scan the contents of the newspaper.
6. Show students the six categories you have created. Ask each student to find her favorite part of the newspaper and write the name of that part on her reproducible.
7. Explain that each student should stand up and move to the area of the room where you've placed the card for his favorite part of the paper. He should bring his reproducible and a pencil.
8. Ask each student to write on his reproducible the name of another student who has chosen the same part of the newspaper as his favorite.
9. Ask students from each group to tell the class what their favorite part of the newspaper is and why. When you get to the students who chose "other," be sure to find out what specific parts of the newspaper they enjoy.
10. Read aloud a piece from the newspaper (e.g., the weather forecast, a sports article, a listing for a used truck for sale).
11. Explain that each student should turn to the first group of boxes on the reproducible and use a yellow crayon to shade the box that shows where that item appeared in the newspaper.
12. Ask students to move near the card showing where they might find what you read (e.g., if you read aloud a movie review, students would walk to the Movies/TV card).
13. Repeat with items from other parts of the paper.
14. Discuss responses as a class.

# LISTEN UP!

1. Write down the name of your favorite part of the newspaper.

_____

2. Write down the name of another person whose favorite part of the paper

is the same as yours._____

3. Your teacher is going to read some pieces from the newspaper. With a yellow crayon, shade in the box that lists the part of the newspaper where you think you would find each piece.

| ARTICLE #1 | |
|---|---|
| Comics | Classifieds |
| Sports | Movies/TV |
| Weather | Other |

| ARTICLE #4 | |
|---|---|
| Comics | Classifieds |
| Sports | Movies/TV |
| Weather | Other |

| ARTICLE #2 | |
|---|---|
| Comics | Classifieds |
| Sports | Movies/TV |
| Weather | Other |

| ARTICLE #5 | |
|---|---|
| Comics | Classifieds |
| Sports | Movies/TV |
| Weather | Other |

| ARTICLE #3 | |
|---|---|
| Comics | Classifieds |
| Sports | Movies/TV |
| Weather | Other |

| ARTICLE #6 | |
|---|---|
| Comics | Classifieds |
| Sports | Movies/TV |
| Weather | Other |

# Where's That?

Once your students have become properly excited about using newspapers, challenge them to see if they can find specific items in the newspaper and identify different elements of the text (e.g., letters, words, and authors' names). In that way, this activity functions a lot like a scavenger hunt. To make it more fun for all of your logical/mathematical learners, follow up the highlighting by asking students to add the number of letters highlighted in a headline to the number of words in the lead sentence.

## WHAT YOU NEED

### FOR EACH STUDENT

- **reproducible**
- **newspaper**
- **crayons**
- **pencil**

## OBJECTIVE

Students will demonstrate that they understand concepts about print. They will be able to (1) match oral words to printed words; (2) identify letters, words, and sentences; and (3) identify the title and author of a selection.

## PROCEDURE

1.  Before class, make copies of the reproducible.
2.  In class, hand out all of the materials.
3.  Have each student look at the front page of the newspaper.
4.  Tell students you will read the name of the newspaper and the date. Ask students to highlight what you say with a yellow crayon.
5.  Explain to students that headlines are the titles of newspaper stories and that they are usually written in bigger, darker letters.
6.  Ask each student to choose a story and use a pencil to draw a box around each word in the headline.
7.  Ask each student to draw a circle, again with a pencil, around each letter of one word in the headline.
8.  Explain to students that the name of the author of a newspaper story usually follows the headline and appears in smaller print.

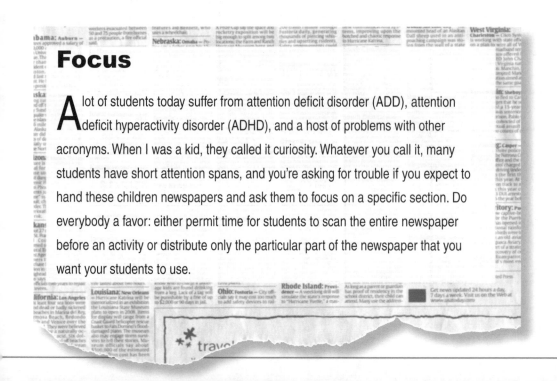

## Focus

A lot of students today suffer from attention deficit disorder (ADD), attention deficit hyperactivity disorder (ADHD), and a host of problems with other acronyms. When I was a kid, they called it curiosity. Whatever you call it, many students have short attention spans, and you're asking for trouble if you expect to hand these children newspapers and ask them to focus on a specific section. Do everybody a favor: either permit time for students to scan the entire newspaper before an activity or distribute only the particular part of the newspaper that you want your students to use.

9. Ask each student to highlight with an orange crayon the name of the author of the newspaper story she's chosen.

10. Ask each student to underline with a pencil the first sentence in the selected newspaper story. Explain to students that the first sentence of a news story is called the "lead."

11. Have each student repeat the procedure with one of the stories on the reproducible and then answer the questions there. (Note that it's perfectly accurate for a student to mark up either story.)

12. Allow students to share their responses with one another and as a class.

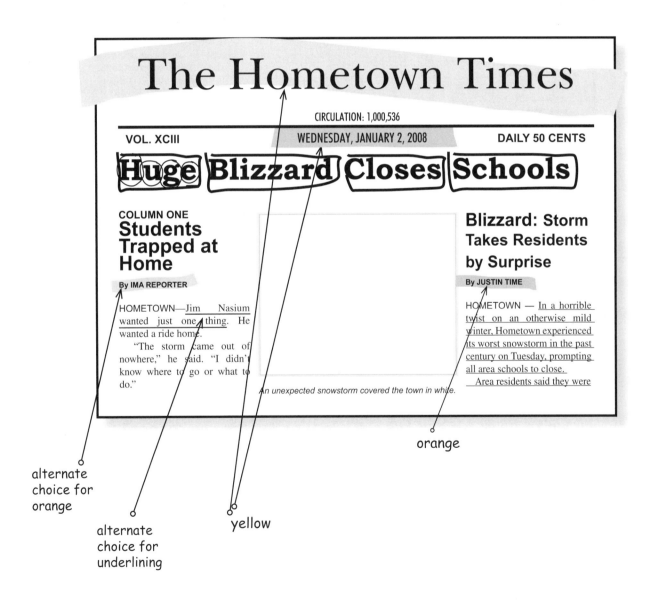

alternate choice for orange

alternate choice for underlining

yellow

orange

# WHERE'S THAT?

## The Hometown Times

CIRCULATION: 1,000,536

| VOL. XCIII | WEDNESDAY, JANUARY 2, 2008 | DAILY 50 CENTS |

# Huge Blizzard Closes Schools

COLUMN ONE

### Students Trapped at Home

By IMA REPORTER

HOMETOWN—Jim Nasium wanted just one thing. He wanted a ride home.

"The storm came out of nowhere," he said. "I didn't know where to go or what to do."

*An unexpected snowstorm covered the town in white.*

### Blizzard: Storm Takes Residents by Surprise

By JUSTIN TIME

HOMETOWN — In a horrible twist on an otherwise mild winter, Hometown experienced its worst snowstorm in the past century on Tuesday, prompting all area schools to close.

Area residents said they were

---

1. What is the name of the newspaper in the picture above?

_____

2. What is the date of the newspaper?

_____

3. Can you write down a word from a headline in this newspaper?

_____

4. Who is the author of the newspaper story you've chosen?

_____

# Surfin' the Newspaper

Whenever my mechanic explains a problem to me, I tend to hear, "Blah, blah, blah . . . $399." Virtually every aspect of our lives has its own unique vocabulary, and newspapers are no exception. Don't let your students get lost in newspaper terminology. Instead, build their confidence by helping them understand the "language" of newspapers. Here's a way to provide students with the practice they need to make newspaper reading an effortless routine rather than an intimidating task. Note that this works best with a large daily newspaper. If that's not what your class is typically using, try going to the Internet. Most major dailies have Internet editions from which you can download excerpts for free (see page 137 for specific Web sites).

## WHAT YOU NEED

### FOR EACH STUDENT

- **reproducible**
- **newspaper**
- **crayons**
- **pencil**

## OBJECTIVE

Students will demonstrate knowledge of newspaper-related vocabulary and use headings and indexes to locate information in text.

## PROCEDURE

1. Before class, make copies of the reproducible.
2. In class, ask students how many of them read the newspaper. Ask the newspaper readers what their favorite parts of the newspaper are.
3. Tell students that since they will be looking at newspapers daily, it is important for them to become familiar with the "language of newspapers" and how to find different types of information in a newspaper.
4. Hand out the newspapers.
5. Have students scan the newspaper, looking over the front page, sports section, comics, and other sections.
6. Instruct students to turn to the front page of the newspaper.
7. Discuss with students what jargon is. Ask them to brainstorm jargon that they use with friends, hear in the classroom, and hear on television and in real life. Explain how newspapers use jargon as well.
8. Make sure everyone has crayons and a pencil.
9. Introduce the list of newspaper terms included in the reproducible. Explain the terms to students and tell them that they will be scanning the newspaper to find examples of each term.
10. Ask each student to follow the instructions on the reproducible, working with a partner to complete the final section. Explain that each pair should be prepared to share their results with the class.
11. Allow each pair of students to share their findings with another pair.
12. Ask students to share their ideas as a class.
13. Discuss any questions students may have.

## EXTRA! EXTRA!

This activity easily lends itself to addressing multiple intelligences. Allow some students to classify different words as headlines, authors, etc. Have others create maps of where a reader would find different information on the front page.

Finally, to reinforce newspaper jargon with students and make them feel comfortable using it, allow small groups to create skits in which they act like newspaper reporters and editors using newspaper terms to create a newspaper.

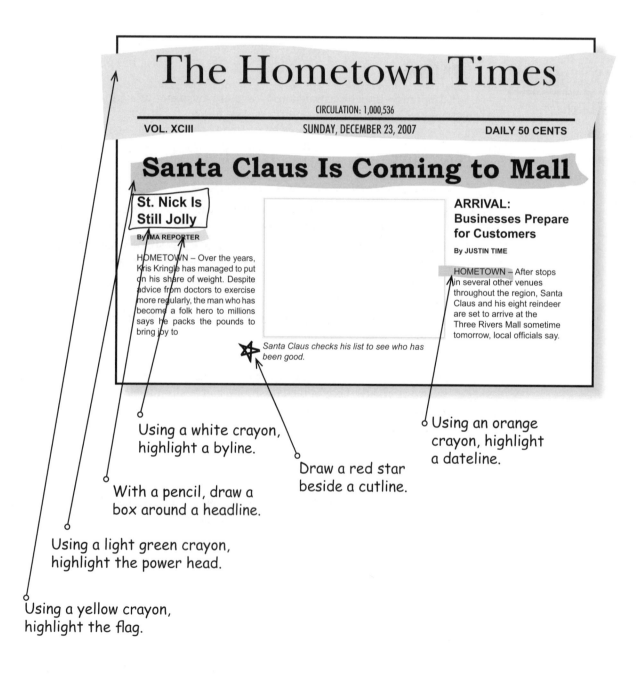

# The Hometown Times

CIRCULATION: 1,000,536

VOL. XCIII                SUNDAY, DECEMBER 23, 2007                DAILY 50 CENTS

## Santa Claus Is Coming to Mall

### St. Nick Is Still Jolly

By IMA REPORTER

HOMETOWN – Over the years, Kris Kringle has managed to put on his share of weight. Despite advice from doctors to exercise more regularly, the man who has become a folk hero to millions says he packs the pounds to bring joy to

*Santa Claus checks his list to see who has been good.*

### ARRIVAL: Businesses Prepare for Customers

By JUSTIN TIME

HOMETOWN – After stops in several other venues throughout the region, Santa Claus and his eight reindeer are set to arrive at the Three Rivers Mall sometime tomorrow, local officials say.

Using a white crayon, highlight a byline.

Draw a red star beside a cutline.

Using an orange crayon, highlight a dateline.

With a pencil, draw a box around a headline.

Using a light green crayon, highlight the power head.

Using a yellow crayon, highlight the flag.

# Surfin' the Newspaper

## NEWSPAPER TERMS

**FLAG**—the top of the front page, including the name of the newspaper, the date, the circulation, and the cost

**BYLINE**—the name of the person who wrote the story

**CUTLINE OR CAPTION**—descriptive text next to a photo or drawing

**DATELINE**—the location where the story took place

**HEADLINE**—large type above the story that captures the reader's attention

**POWER HEAD**—the biggest, boldest headline

**TOP STORY**—the story with the biggest headline, running "above the fold"

**INDEX**—the table of contents, informing readers where they can find specific parts of the newspaper

**LEAD**—the opening line(s) of a news story, usually including who, what, when, where, why, and how

1. Using a yellow crayon, highlight the flag of your newspaper. Copy the words of the flag here.

_____

2. Using a white crayon, highlight a byline. Copy the byline here.

_____

3. Draw a red star beside a cutline.

4. Using an orange crayon, highlight a dateline. Copy the dateline here.

_____

5. Using your pencil, draw a box around a headline.

6. Using a light green crayon, highlight the power head.

7. What is your favorite item in the newspaper (for example, sports scores or a particular comic strip)? _____

_____

8. With a partner, find the newspaper's index. Can each of you find your favorite part of the newspaper in the index? Write down the name of your favorite section. _____

9. BONUS: With your partner, underline any examples you can find of a top story or a lead in another section of the paper. Share your examples with another pair of students.

# Scavenger Hunt

The more proficient your students become at finding items in newspapers, the more likely it is that they will read newspapers. This activity builds student confidence in using newspapers by providing further opportunities to practice. Students enjoy showing off their newspaper skills as they compete against one another to find items quickly. This also works as something of a written version of Simon Says, as students get to show off how well they follow directions.

## WHAT YOU NEED

### FOR EACH STUDENT

- reproducible
- newspaper
- pencil

## OBJECTIVE

Students will follow one- and two-step instructions.

## PROCEDURE

1. Before class, modify the reproducible, if necessary, to make it appropriate for the newspaper you're using. Then make copies of the reproducible.

2. In class, ask students to work in teams of three.

3. Tell students that they are going to have a scavenger hunt. On this scavenger hunt, they will be searching for specific kinds of items in the newspaper.

4. Remind students that different sections of the newspaper are often lettered. This is important, as students need to know that if they come across an item in the A section of the newspaper, they must record the page number as A-13, rather than just 13.

5. Hand out all of the materials.

6. Instruct students to look through their newspapers to locate each type of item listed in the reproducible. Explain that they should write, in the appropriate box on the right-hand side of the reproducible, the page number where they find each item.

7. Explain that you want each team to identify as many examples of each item as they can, but that they must find at least one example of each.

8. Challenge students to try to be the first team to complete the scavenger hunt with all of the items correctly identified.

## EXTRA! EXTRA!

The point of this activity is to see if students can follow directions and familiarize themselves with different items in the newspaper. Another way to ensure that students can identify these items is to facilitate a "jigsaw" activity in which each student chooses to become an expert on one of five items. (As there are twenty items on the list, you can chunk this activity into four sections.) Then group together experts on *different* items so that each expert can teach the rest of her small group what she has learned. (For example, the index expert would explain the index to others who have learned about the weather section or obituaries.) This is a great differentiation tool because it allows everyone to be an expert on something.

# SCAVENGER HUNT

| Item | Page in Newspaper |
|---|---|
| 1. The power head (headline for the top story on the front page) | |
| 2. A sports photo | |
| 3. An obituary | |
| 4. The weather forecast | |
| 5. A crossword puzzle | |
| 6. A comic strip | |
| 7. An editorial cartoon | |
| 8. The newspaper index | |
| 9. A box score | |
| 10. A byline | |
| 11. A dateline | |
| 12. An advertisement photo | |
| 13. A help wanted ad | |
| 14. A movie ad | |
| 15. The name of the newspaper's editor | |
| 16. A story with bad news | |
| 17. A story with good news | |
| 18. A picture of a columnist | |
| 19. The name of the newspaper | |
| 20. The cost of the newspaper | |

# Say, Act & Draw

Comic strips are just about the easiest starting point for drawing students' attention to newspapers. They're perfect for getting students thinking about the beginning, middle, and end of a story as the students recount selected comics in their own words. This activity shows students how they can discuss what they read in newspapers in the same way they discuss their favorite TV shows, movies, and video games. It's also the perfect multiple-intelligence activity, because it allows students to show what they know in so many different ways.

## WHAT YOU NEED

### FOR EACH STUDENT

- **reproducible**
- **newspaper**
- **crayons**
- **pencil**

## OBJECTIVE

Students will retell, paraphrase, and explain what a speaker has said.

## PROCEDURE

1. Before class, make copies of the reproducible.
2. In class, tell your students that a good story always has a beginning, middle, and end.
3. Ask students to close their eyes while you read them an article from the newspaper. Ask each student to picture in his head what's happening in the story.
4. Ask students to buddy up. Explain that in each pair, one student should tell the other what the story was about.
5. Allow one or two student volunteers to act out the story in front of the class. Review the beginning, middle, and end of the story.
6. Hand out the newspapers and direct students to turn to the comics.
7. Ask them if they can figure out the story of a comic strip just by looking at the pictures.
8. Ask students if they remember the pictures that came into their heads when you read the newspaper story aloud.
9. Make sure everyone has crayons and a pencil.
10. Explain that, in the first row of boxes on the reproducible, each student should draw a comic strip that shows what happened in the story you just read.
11. Ask students to think of their own stories. Remind students that a good story has a beginning, middle, and end.
12. Instruct each student to draw a comic strip based on his story in the middle row of boxes on the reproducible.
13. Ask each student to tell his story to his partner without showing the partner his comic strip. Encourage him to tell his story in his own way (e.g., through drawing, singing, acting, graphing).
14. Instruct each partner to draw a comic strip in the bottom row of boxes on his own copy of the reproducible showing what he heard.
15. Then have the partner tell the story back to the student. Encourage partners to act out the stories as they retell them.
16. Ask students how accurately their partners retold their stories.
17. Have students swap roles and repeat the process.

# SAY, ACT & DRAW

# Word Analysis & Fluency

Many young children benefit from learning simple exercises that develop their knowledge of phonemic awareness and phonics. Teachers often confuse these two concepts by overcomplicating them (which is easy to do, given the number of fancy education terms thrown around by researchers, experts, and policymakers). Put simply, phonemic awareness deals with recognizing the sounds of language, while phonics is taking those sounds and associating them with the written symbols we call letters. First-grade teachers, in particular, feel the burden of familiarizing students with concepts such as phonograms, onsets, rimes, and plenty of other fancy terms used in teaching the "science" of reading. It seems that anything a student does not know is blamed on first-grade teachers, and that is why I sympathize so much with my comrades in grade 1.

Teaching phonemic awareness and phonics to my first, second, and third graders did not exactly thrill me. (Yes, second- and third-grade teachers often have to reinforce students' phonemic awareness and phonics skills, as some students forget these skills, others never learned them, and still others completely disregard them so they can go back to eating paste and looking "creepy" in the back of the classroom). But a lack of enthusiasm on this front is dangerous, as you cannot expect your students to get excited about something that does not spark your passion and enthusiasm. If you are yawning and nodding off in the middle of your own lesson, there is a problem. The challenge for teachers is to find a way to bring to life a topic or concept that does not exactly stimulate us. Newspapers helped me enjoy teaching phonics and phonemic awareness. I'm convinced that they can do the same for you.

Most states' English/language-arts standards for word analysis and fluency for grades 1–3 require students to understand the basic features of reading (e.g., concepts about print). They also require that students be able to select letter patterns and know how to translate them into spoken language by using phonics, syllabication, and word parts. Students need to be able to apply this knowledge to achieve fluency in both oral and silent reading. The following mini-lessons are meant to stimulate students' interest in reading newspapers and to direct their attention to the relationship between print features and the sounds of language.

## Create a Classroom Newspaper

People learn best through experience, and nothing will assist your students' understanding of newspapers better than allowing them to create their own classroom newspaper. They'll love sharing their paper with one another, their parents, the school, and the community. A number of great books and Internet materials are available to show you how to create an outstanding classroom newspaper. My students and I enjoyed creating newspapers that included sports stories (e.g., recess kickball reports and scores), advice columns (e.g., "Dear Julietta"), and classroom special-interest items (e.g., which group led the week in attendance).

# Shortcuts

**W**e want students to understand common abbreviations, and newspapers are filled with examples—from the news section ("Pres." for "President") to the events section ("Sun." for "Sunday"), to the classifieds ("St." for "Street"). Here's a way to get students to focus on them.

## WHAT YOU NEED

### FOR EACH STUDENT

- **scissors**
- **glue stick**
- **pencil**

### FOR EACH GROUP

- **newspaper**
- **index cards**
- **manila envelope**

## OBJECTIVE

Students will recognize common abbreviations (e.g., Jan., Sun., Mr., St.).

## PROCEDURE

1. Ask students to work in groups of four or five.
2. Hand out the newspapers and index cards.
3. Make sure everyone has scissors, a glue stick, and a pencil.
4. Tell each group to divide the sections of the newspaper among the group members.
5. Explain that each student should cut out abbreviations from the newspaper and glue each one on a separate index card.
6. Add that if a student knows other abbreviations that she can't find in the newspaper, she should write those abbreviations on other index cards.
7. Have students turn each card over and write what the abbreviation stands for on the back.
8. Ask each group to discuss these questions:

   a. What was the most common abbreviation your group found in the newspaper?

   b. What section of the newspaper contains the most abbreviations?

   c. What abbreviations do you know that you did not find in the newspaper?
9. Ask students to swap cards with other groups and practice guessing what each abbreviation stands for.
10. Review the cards as a class to make sure the answers are correct.
11. Give each group a manila envelope and instruct the group to place all of their cards in the envelope.
12. Place the envelopes in a center so students can continue to practice.

## EXTRA! EXTRA!

You can enhance this "make and take" center by asking students to make a set of cards with just abbreviations and another set with just the full words those abbreviations represent. Tell students to put all of the cards facedown and play a game like Concentration, matching the abbreviation cards with their spelled-out equivalents.

For further practice, encourage students to create word finds and matching puzzles that review abbreviations and the words they stand for.

# Seek & Sound Out

This activity allows students to practice sounding out words in the newspaper every day, thus providing them with meaningful context and real-life reading experience while also teaching them to distinguish a variety of sounds.

## WHAT YOU NEED

### FOR EACH STUDENT

- **reproducible**
- **newspaper**
- **yellow crayon**
- **pencil**

## OBJECTIVE

Students will distinguish initial, medial, and final sounds in single-syllable words.

## PROCEDURE

1. Before class, make copies of the reproducible.
2. In class, hand out the newspapers and have students look at the front page.
3. Remind students that the "flag" is always at the top of the front page and includes information such as the name of the newspaper, the date, the circulation, and the cost.
4. Also remind students that headlines are the titles of newspaper stories and that headlines are usually written in bigger, darker letters than the stories.
5. Make sure everyone has a yellow crayon and a pencil.
6. Tell students you want them to highlight with the crayon as many single-syllable words as they can find within the flag and headlines on the front page. Mark up one headline together as a class, then allow each student to mark up her own newspaper.
7. Explain that each student is to draw lines separating the distinct sounds in the words that she's highlighted. Choose one word from a headline and mark it up together as a class. Then allow students to practice independently with their own newspapers.
8. Hand out the copies of the reproducible.
9. Tell students to answer the questions on the reproducible.
10. Have each student share her work with a partner, following the instructions on the reproducible.

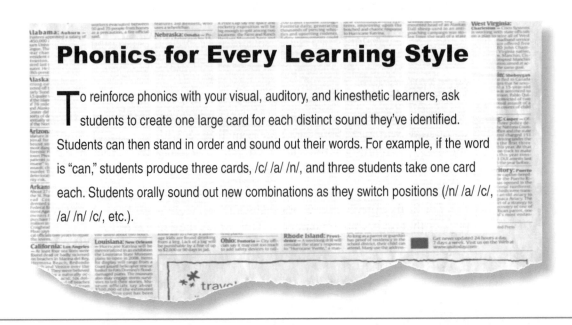

## Phonics for Every Learning Style

To reinforce phonics with your visual, auditory, and kinesthetic learners, ask students to create one large card for each distinct sound they've identified. Students can then stand in order and sound out their words. For example, if the word is "can," students produce three cards, /c/ /a/ /n/, and three students take one card each. Students orally sound out new combinations as they switch positions (/n/ /a/ /c/, /a/ /n/ /c/, etc.).

# SEEK & SOUND OUT

## The Hometown Times

CIRCULATION: 1,000,536

VOL. XCIII — MONDAY, MARCH 10, 2008 — DAILY 50 CENTS

### Local Team Wins Pennant!

**COLUMN ONE**

#### All-Stars Triumph

By IMA REPORTER

HOMETOWN—The only thing Bill Ding knew for sure was that he was getting an ice-cream sundae. "My parents told me if I got a hit, then they'd take me to Dairy King," he said. He got his ice cream.

*The third-grade all-stars hoist their trophy.*

**Manager:**
*"These Kids Had Heart!"*

By JUSTIN TIME

HOMETOWN — Playing against their toughest competition of the year, Hometown's third-grade all-star team won the league title on Sunday with a dramatic 5–4 come-from-behind victory at Veterans Field.

1. Using a yellow crayon, highlight as many single-syllable words as you can find in the flag and headlines above. Please copy the words below.

_____

_____

_____

_____

2. Go back to the words you wrote down. Use your pencil to draw lines separating the letters that show different sounds.

3. Show your work to a partner. Did you both highlight the same words? Can you sound out each word orally?

# Compounding Interest

Newspapers provide students with all kinds of examples of commonly used compound words and contractions. This activity allows students to quickly identify which compound words and contractions occur the most frequently and where. Students can then compare these words with the high-frequency compound words they see on their word wall.

## WHAT YOU NEED

### FOR EACH STUDENT

- **reproducible**
- **newspaper**
- **crayons**
- **scissors**
- **glue stick**
- **pencil**

## OBJECTIVE

Students will be able to identify compound words and contractions.

## PROCEDURE

1.  Before class, make copies of the reproducible.
2.  In class, review the concept of compound words with students.
3.  Hand out the newspapers and have students look at the front page.
4.  Make sure every student has crayons, scissors, a glue stick, and a pencil.
5.  Ask each student to find five compound words on the front page and to highlight each one with a yellow crayon.
6.  Review contractions with students.
7.  Ask each student to find five contractions on the front page and to highlight each contraction with an orange crayon.
8.  Hand out the copies of the reproducible.
9.  Tell students to follow the instructions on the reproducible.
10. Ask each student to share his story with a partner.
11. Allow volunteers to share their stories with the class.

## EXTRA! EXTRA!

To extend this activity, take the compound words and contractions that your students find in their newspapers and play a game called Backseat. Tell students that compound words are words that get along and sit nicely beside each other and that contractions feel squished and get tangled up. Create large cards with one word on each, then give one card to each student. Have each student look for someone who has a word that goes with her own word to create either a compound word or a contraction. For instance, "base" looks for "ball," and "I" looks for "have." When a student finds a matching word (it is possible for students to find more than one match), the pair either sit next to each other to form a compound word or sit on top of each other to form a contraction. This is a great way to get kids out of their seats and to entice your kinesthetic learners.

# COMPOUNDING INTEREST

1. Cut out the compound words and contractions you highlighted in your newspaper. Glue them in the boxes where they belong.

Compound Words

Contractions

2. Write your own news story using at least two of the compound words and two of the contractions you glued in the boxes. Your story must be at least four sentences long.

_____

_____

_____

_____

_____

_____

# Long- & Short-Vowel Mix & Match

One of the reasons students enjoy reading newspapers is that newspapers are written in clear, concise language. This activity encourages students to show off their decoding skills and sound out words found in newspapers.

## WHAT YOU NEED

### FOR EACH STUDENT

- **reproducible**
- **newspaper**
- **crayons**
- **scissors**
- **pencil**

### FOR THE CLASS

- **markers**
- **poster board**

## OBJECTIVE

Students will distinguish long and short vowel sounds.

## PROCEDURE

1. Before class, make copies of the reproducible.
2. As a class, review the difference between long vowel sounds and short vowel sounds.
3. Hand out the newspapers.
4. Make sure everyone has crayons, scissors, and a pencil.
5. Tell students they have two minutes. In that time, they are to choose any headline in the newspaper and highlight the words in the headline, using a yellow crayon for words that have a long vowel sound and an orange crayon for words that have a short vowel sound. If a word contains both long and short vowel sounds, students should use both colors.
6. Ask students to cut out their highlighted headlines.
7. As a class, brainstorm a list of the words students found that have long and short vowel sounds. Record the brainstorming on the blackboard. Orally review which words have short vowel sounds and which words have long vowel sounds.
8. Make sure you have at least two examples of each vowel sound.
9. Hand out the copies of the reproducible and ask students to copy each word from the class blackboard in the appropriate box on the reproducible.
10. Allow students to pair off and share their categorizations with their partners.
11. Ask students to share with their partners the other examples they found of headline words with long and short vowel sounds.
12. Ask students to work together to copy their words onto a single sheet of poster board to help the class remember each separate long and short vowel sound (e.g., "Short *a:* cat, handcuffs, bad, lack").

## EXTRA! EXTRA!

You can also have fun with short- and long-vowel sounds by creating "hink pinks" and "hinkie pinkies." Hink pinks are pairs of single-syllable words with the same long or short vowel sound (e.g., fat cat, late mate, black shack). Hinkie pinkies are pairs of two-syllable words with the same long or short vowel sounds (e.g., handy candy, flower shower, Viking biking). Ask students to see if they can find photos in the newspaper that could be described with a hink pink or hinkie pinkie caption. Advertisement photos work especially well.

# LONG- & SHORT-VOWEL MIX & MATCH

| a | Short Vowels<br><br>(examples: cat, wet, thin, dog, fun) | e |
|---|---|---|
| i | o | u |

| a | Long Vowels<br><br>(examples: make, green, write, boat, use) | e |
|---|---|---|
| i | o | u |

# Word Family Circus

There are ways to develop students' phonemic awareness and phonics without sacrificing student interest. Newspapers are wonderful environmental print sources for phonograms, and this activity also draws student attention to common phonograms they see on cereal boxes, food wrappers, and the like.

Note that you do not have to cover all of the phonograms in one day. It may be easier to focus on just a few phonograms and make this an ongoing daily activity. It takes a while to develop the phonogram cards initially. Once the cards are created, however, you can review the cards for five or ten minutes a day and cover a number of objectives, such as letter and sound identification, word families, and so on.

## WHAT YOU NEED

### FOR EACH STUDENT

- **newspaper**
- **scissors**
- **pencil**

### FOR EACH GROUP

- **index cards**

### FOR THE CLASS

- **pocket chart**

## OBJECTIVE

Students will generate sounds from letters and letter patterns, including consonant blends and long- and short-vowel patterns (i.e., phonograms), and blend those sounds into recognizable words, reading common word families (e.g., *-ack, -ake,-ink*).

## PROCEDURE

1. Explain to students that 37 phonograms (aka word families, such as *-an, -at, -est*) form more than 500 high-frequency words. Provide examples.

2. As a class, take any phonogram (e.g., *-est*). Brainstorm words that end in that phonogram (e.g., best, chest, nest, test). Look through the newspaper and try to find words in news headlines and advertisement headings that include that particular phonogram.

3. Ask students to work in groups of four or five.

4. Assign each group four or five phonograms.

5. Hand out the newspapers.

6. Make sure everyone has scissors and a pencil.

7. Ask the groups to look through the headlines and advertisements in their newspapers to find words that include their assigned phonograms.

8. Tell them to cut out each of these words and group them by word family.

9. Add that they should copy each group of words onto an index card, then write the appropriate phonogram on the back of the card.

10. After the groups are finished, return to working with the whole class.

11. Ask each group to present one of their phonogram cards to the class. Ask students if they can think of additional words that belong to that word family.

12. Encourage students to find common phonograms in other environmental print that they can cut out and copy onto the index card for each word family.

13. Use the index cards and a pocket chart as a center in which students can practice classifying phonograms.

## EXTRA! EXTRA!

For your musical/rhythmic learners, create classroom "raps" that focus on specific phonograms. For example, my students and I would review single-syllable -*at* words by reciting a rap they created: "That fat cat is not all that. / He sat on a rat on the welcome mat. / He grabbed my hat and never stopped to chat. / That fat cat sure is a rat."

## Common Phonograms

| | | | | |
|---|---|---|---|---|
| -ab | -ank | -ick | -ip | -uck |
| -ack | -ap | -ight | -ob | -ug |
| -ag | -at | -ill | -ock | -um |
| -ail | -ay | -im | -op | -unk |
| -ain | -eed | -in | -ore | -y |
| -ake | -ell | -ine | -ot | |
| -am | -est | -ing | -out | |
| -an | -ew | -ink | -ow | |

# Silly Syllables

**L**ife is all a matter of semantics. I met a veteran kindergarten teacher who told me she has never assigned homework in forty years. Instead, she assigns "home games." Developing students' ability to decode words is much more interesting for them (and for you) when you turn it into a game. This activity encourages students to read the comics and look for words with different numbers of syllables. It also includes a twist for your logical/mathematical learners.

## WHAT YOU NEED

### FOR EACH STUDENT

- **crayons**
- **pencil**

### FOR EACH PAIR

- **reproducible**
- **newspaper**
- **business envelope**

## OBJECTIVE

Students will decode single- and multisyllable words and recognize and apply rules of syllabication.

## PROCEDURE

1. Before class, make copies of the reproducible.
2. In class, review how to sound out words by syllables.
3. Point out to students that they can practice sounding out words as they look at the newspaper every day.
4. Make sure everyone has crayons and a pencil.
5. Ask students to work in pairs, and give each pair a newspaper.
6. Ask each pair to find the comics in the newspaper and to look at the words in the comics.
7. Ask each pair to choose one comic strip to work with.
8. Give each pair an envelope and a copy of the reproducible.
9. Explain that each pair should copy all of the single-syllable words in their comic strip into the first set of boxes on the reproducible, all of the two-syllable words into the second set of boxes, and all of the three-syllable words into the third set of boxes.
10. Allow each pair to show their reproducible boxes to another pair of students. Tell the pairs to swap reproducibles and double-check that their classmates have grouped the words correctly.
11. Challenge students by posing word problems related to single- and multisyllable words. For example, ask each pair to subtract the number of one-syllable words they've found from the number of two-syllable words they've found. Then direct the pair to add that number to their count of three-syllable words.

---

REPRODUCIBLE

### SILLY SYLLABLES

| 1-Syllable Words | |
|---|---|
| Give | to |
| me | hold |
| the | it |
| I | |

| 2-Syllable Words | |
|---|---|
| football | |
| promise | |
| steady | |
| | |

| 3-Syllable Words | |
|---|---|
| | |
| | |
| | |
| | |

12. Ask students to cut out each individual box (each word) on the reproducible and put all of the cutout words in the envelope.

13. Place all of the envelopes in a center.

14. Have students shuffle the cutouts from an envelope and practice classifying the words by the number of syllables they contain.

## EXTRA! EXTRA!

Another way to encourage students to pay attention to the number of syllables in words is to create bulletin boards for one-, two-, and three-syllable words. Allow students to cut words out of their newspapers and glue them on bulletin boards. This gives you an instant word wall, and you can reward students with special incentives for every twenty-five words they add to the bulletin boards. Incentives could include things such as cartoon read-alouds (you read comics aloud to the class), coupon clipping (many students love to clip coupons to take home to their parents), and extra newspaper reading time.

### Sell Newspapers

Your enthusiasm matters! Get excited about newspapers, and your students will catch that excitement. Constantly point out cool features in the newspaper. Keep a list of students' favorite sections, and give out special newspaper clippings to two or three students each day. You will be amazed by how excited a student will be when you hand him a newspaper and say, "Joe, I know how much you enjoy the sports page, and I thought you'd love this article on tomorrow's big World Cup game." I found that there was a 100 percent likelihood that a student would read a newspaper clipping that I promoted in this manner.

# SILLY SYLLABLES

| 1-Syllable Words | |
| --- | --- |
| | |
| | |
| | |
| | |

| 2-Syllable Words | |
| --- | --- |
| | |
| | |
| | |
| | |

| 3-Syllable Words | |
| --- | --- |
| | |
| | |
| | |
| | |

# CHAPTER 4

# Vocabulary Development

When I ask adults how they were taught vocabulary in school, they invariably describe the same routine: they received a list of twenty vocabulary words on Monday, took a quiz on Friday, and forgot the words by Saturday. Also, their teachers encouraged them to look up unfamiliar words in the dictionary. I'd like to offer a more efficient use of your time when dealing with vocabulary instruction: hand your students newspapers.

Newspapers are a fantastic resource for teaching students how to determine word meanings through context. News articles, in particular, expose students to a wonderful array of strategies for guessing a word's meaning, from repetition and clarification to photographs and charts. The newspaper also benefits students' vocabulary-guessing skills, as students are exposed to stories that interest them on subjects they already know something about. This means that if your boys want to read only sports stories, let them; even the most basic sports story provides assistance in clarifying the meanings of words.

As part of most states' English/language-arts standards for vocabulary development for grades 1–3, students need to develop extensive vocabulary through meaningful experiences with text. They also need to be able to use vocabulary to clearly describe ideas, feelings, and experiences. The following mini-lessons are meant to hasten students' vocabulary growth by exposing them to high-frequency words and standard American English (academic language) in ways that stimulate their interest and their newspaper reading habits.

## Foster Curiosity

Always stay one step ahead of your students. One of my greatest joys in teaching young students was seeing their excitement with new things (in contrast to my middle-school students, who often looked at me as if I were a virus). You can keep young students interested in anything by adding an element of surprise. For example, tell the kids something like this: "After we finish our weather haiku poems, I will show you something in the newspaper that will make your mouth water." (It will be a recipe in the food section for chocolate chip cookies.) Or you might say, "I saw an article about the world's richest man, and I do not remember where I read it." Of course, you remember perfectly well where you read it, but your students will always be anxious to help you with your dilemma.

# Dull to Rich

**P**aint strips from your local paint or home improvement store are perfect for this activity, because they serve as a reference point for students converting dull words (e.g., said) to progressively richer words (e.g., expressed, commented, exclaimed, shouted). Dull words are often high-frequency words, and this strategy encourages students to think about replacing those terms with more interesting ones in their writing.

If you do not have paint strips, you can still have students complete this activity, but the strips make the point more concretely. Ask the manager at any paint or home improvement store to donate the paint strips. You will be amazed by how supportive parents and community members are when you do two things: (1) ask and (2) write a thank-you note. Besides, the more you get your community invested in your students' success, the more your students will get the message that it is their responsibility to try their hardest to succeed. Let your students know as often as possible how important they are to their community.

## WHAT YOU NEED

### FOR EACH STUDENT

- **reproducible**
- **newspaper**
- **paint strip**
- **pencil**
- **crayons**

## OBJECTIVE

Students will identify and explain high-frequency words that have synonyms.

## PROCEDURE

1. Before class, make copies of the reproducible.
2. In class, hand out the newspapers.
3. Ask students to scan stories and headlines throughout the newspaper and look for high-frequency words. (I call these "dull words" because they are overused.)
4. Show students one of the paint strips and point out how the colors deepen from dull, light colors to rich, dark colors.
5. Give each student a paint strip, just to illustrate the point, and a copy of the reproducible. Make sure everyone has a pencil and crayons.
6. Ask each student to find a high-frequency (dull) word in a newspaper headline and write it in the first left-hand box on the reproducible.
7. Explain that students should then list richer words with the same meaning in each box to the right of the original word.

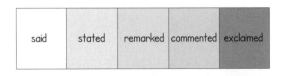

8. Ask students to repeat the process in the remaining strips on the reproducible.
9. Tell students to color each box, going from light to dark as they move from left to right in each row. Explain that the word in each box must be readable after the student has colored the box.
10. Allow students to compete to see who can come up with the most synonyms for any dull word.
11. Challenge students to find newspaper articles that use the synonyms they name.

# DULL TO RICH

| | | | | |
|---|---|---|---|---|
| | | | | |

| | | | | |
|---|---|---|---|---|
| | | | | |

| | | | | |
|---|---|---|---|---|
| | | | | |

| | | | | |
|---|---|---|---|---|
| | | | | |

| | | | | |
|---|---|---|---|---|
| | | | | |

# Category Cutouts

This activity allows students to enjoy the photographs in newspapers. Students create collages while studying specific words and practicing classification skills. This approach may also be used to review different curricular objectives—classifying animals (science), foods (health), places (social studies), and so on.

## WHAT YOU NEED

### FOR EACH STUDENT

- **newspaper**
- **scissors**
- **glue stick**

### FOR EACH GROUP

- **butcher paper**

### FOR THE TEACHER

- **marker**

## OBJECTIVE

Students will classify grade-appropriate categories of words (e.g., animals, foods, toys).

## PROCEDURE

1. Before class, use a marker to divide each group's sheet of butcher paper into four sections. Label one section "animals," one "foods," one "people," and one "places."
2. Hand out the newspapers.
3. Make sure everyone has scissors and a glue stick.
4. Ask each student, working independently, to find photos in the newspaper that fit into each category and to cut out those photos.
5. Ask students to form groups of four or five.
6. Give each group one sheet of butcher paper.
7. Ask each group to glue all of their photos under the appropriate labels.
8. Hang each group's sheet of butcher paper on a bulletin board.
9. Review each group's work as a class. Check to see that all of the photos are classified correctly.

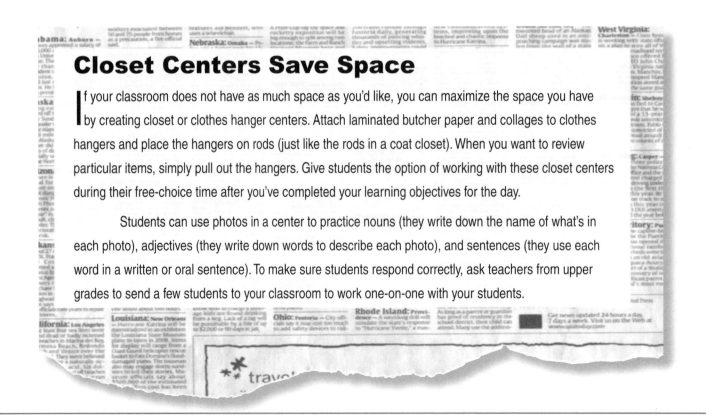

## Closet Centers Save Space

If your classroom does not have as much space as you'd like, you can maximize the space you have by creating closet or clothes hanger centers. Attach laminated butcher paper and collages to clothes hangers and place the hangers on rods (just like the rods in a coat closet). When you want to review particular items, simply pull out the hangers. Give students the option of working with these closet centers during their free-choice time after you've completed your learning objectives for the day.

Students can use photos in a center to practice nouns (they write down the name of what's in each photo), adjectives (they write down words to describe each photo), and sentences (they use each word in a written or oral sentence). To make sure students respond correctly, ask teachers from upper grades to send a few students to your classroom to work one-on-one with your students.

# Word Mansions

**H**ere's a way to assist students in visually remembering tricky words such as antonyms, synonyms, and homonyms. To build in extra interest for your naturalist learners, and to get everybody out of their seats and moving around, take this activity outside. Then let students choose whether they want to create mansions with different rooms for different concepts or parks that are divided into sections for the same purpose.

## WHAT YOU NEED

### FOR EACH STUDENT

- **paper**
- **pencil**
- **newspaper**
- **scissors**
- **glue stick**

### FOR THE CLASS

- **butcher paper**

## OBJECTIVE

Students will use knowledge of antonyms, synonyms, and homonyms to determine the meanings of words.

## PROCEDURE

1. As a class, review what antonyms, synonyms, and homonyms are.
2. Ask students to work in groups of four or five.
3. Hand out all of the materials.
4. Explain that each student should draw on a sheet of paper either a "mansion" with three rooms or a "park" with three sections.
5. Tell each student to cut out a word from a headline anywhere in the newspaper and glue it on the top of her mansion or at the entrance to her park.
6. Explain that the next task is to label one section of the drawing as antonyms, one as synonyms, and one as homonyms. Then ask the student to write in each section all of the appropriate words she can think of to go with the headline word she has chosen.

7. Give the members of each group time to compare the mansions and parks they have created.
8. Allow each group to choose one mansion or park as the members' favorite.
9. Glue the favorites on butcher paper, then ask the class to come up with a name for their wealthy neighborhood of words.

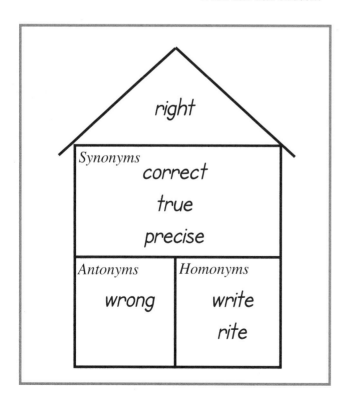

right

*Synonyms*
correct
true
precise

*Antonyms*
wrong

*Homonyms*
write
rite

# Compound Teamwork

**N**ewspapers include a large variety of compound words every day. This activity reinforces the concept that individual words can help students to determine the meanings of longer compound words. It also gives your young artists a chance to strut their stuff.

## WHAT YOU NEED

### FOR EACH STUDENT

- newspaper
- 10 index cards
- scissors
- glue stick
- pencil
- crayons

### FOR THE TEACHER

- box to hold word cards

## OBJECTIVE

Students will use their knowledge of individual words in unknown compound words to predict the meanings of the compound words.

## PROCEDURE

1. As a class, review what a compound word is. Brainstorm examples of compound words.
2. Ask students to work in pairs.
3. Hand out the newspapers.
4. Show students some compound words in the newspaper. Ask them to identify the individual words that make up the compound words and to explain what those words mean when put together.
5. Identify a specific compound word to focus on.
6. With the class, come up with ways to illustrate the individual words that make up that compound word. If the word is "baseball," for example, the class might decide you need to draw a base and a ball.
7. Give each student ten index cards.
8. Make sure everyone has scissors, a glue stick, a pencil, and crayons.
9. Explain that each student should search the newspaper for ten compound words. Point out that the sports and classified sections are good places to start.
10. Tell students to cut out the compound words and glue one on each index card.
11. Ask students to draw a picture of each individual word within that compound word on the back of the index card. Tell them to use a plus sign to separate the pictures that make up each compound word.
12. Allow each student to show her partner the pictures she's drawn and see if the partner can guess the compound words.
13. As a class, look at the compound word cards and use the pictures to determine what each compound word means.
14. Place the compound word cards in a box. Encourage students to use the box as a game during center time, guessing each word based on the pictures.

## EXTRA! EXTRA!

You can also encourage students to practice compound words by turning this game into a board race. Show students the pictures on a card and have them write down the compound word. You can tie this activity into a technology objective  by integrating students' pictures into a PowerPoint quiz, in which students have an allotted time to look at the pictures on each card and try to guess the compound word. Or ask students to create written or oral sentences that use the compound words to ensure that students understand what each word means.

# Pre-fix & Suffix-ed

The benefits of this activity are enormous in terms of students' vocabulary development. Students are more likely to remember words when those words are given a meaningful context, and a word-play skit is a fun way to reinforce students' understanding of words. Anytime your students do not understand what a word means, I suggest that you act it out. (For example, to demonstrate "unhappy," change your expression from happy to sad.) Your students will be more willing to perform in silly routines once they see you do so.

## WHAT YOU NEED

### FOR EACH STUDENT

- **reproducible**
- **newspaper**
- **crayons**
- **pencil**

## OBJECTIVE

Students will know the meanings of simple prefixes (e.g., *over-, un-, re-, pre-*) and suffixes (e.g., *-ing, -ly, -er, -est, -ful*) and use their knowledge of prefixes and suffixes to determine the meanings of words.

## PROCEDURE

1. Before class, make copies of the reproducible.
2. As a class, review specific prefixes and suffixes.
3. Ask students to work in groups of four or five.
4. Give each student a newspaper and a copy of the reproducible.
5. Make sure everyone has crayons and a pencil.
6. Instruct each student to pick one page in his newspaper. Explain that he should scan the page for words containing prefixes and/or suffixes.
7. Explain that each student should use a yellow crayon to highlight words with prefixes and an orange crayon to highlight words with suffixes. If a word has both a prefix and a suffix, he should highlight the beginning of the word in yellow and the end of the word in orange.
8. Ask each student to copy his words with prefixes, suffixes, or both in the appropriate boxes on the reproducible.
9. Instruct the groups to review the prefixes and suffixes their members have found and see which are the most common.
10. Ask group members to discuss and determine the meanings of all the words they've collected.
11. Instruct each group to choose five words that the members believe the entire class should learn.
12. Have each group create and share with the class a word-play skit. Every skit must include acting by all of the group's members and must correctly use all five of the group's words.

## EXTRA! EXTRA!

Good sentences allow readers to determine a word's meaning from the context. Allow students to create silly words with prefixes and suffixes and write or say sentences with their new words. Students may have to write a few sentences to create a context for their words. For example, I had a boy who wrote, "I am anti-homework and pro-recess."

# PRE-FIX & SUFFIX-ED

| Words with Prefixes | Words with Suffixes |
| --- | --- |
|  |  |

| Words with Prefixes and Suffixes |
| --- |
|  |

# Multiple Meanings

This activity encourages students to look for words that have multiple meanings (e.g., "light" could mean "pale," "sunshine," "not heavy," or "to set on fire") and to see if they can determine the words' meanings from the context of the articles in which they find them.

## WHAT YOU NEED

### FOR EACH STUDENT

- **newspaper**
- **4 index cards**
- **scissors**
- **pencil**
- **glue stick**

### FOR THE TEACHER

- **hole punch**
- **book ring**

## OBJECTIVE

Students will identify simple multiple-meaning words.

## PROCEDURE

1. Before class, read the newspaper you're using. Look for something you can use as an example of a word that has multiple meanings (e.g., "ball" could mean "a sphere," "a dance," or "a good time").
2. In class, hand out the newspapers and point out to students examples of how the word you've chosen is used in different ways in the newspaper.
3. As a class, scan the newspaper for examples of other words used in different ways.
4. Hand out the index cards.
5. Make sure everyone has scissors, a pencil, and a glue stick.
6. Explain that students should cut out sentences, headlines, or advertisements that use the same words in different ways.
7. Tell each student to write one multiple-meaning word on an index card.
8. Have the student glue the examples of that word used in different ways on the opposite side of the card.
9. Ask the student to repeat the procedure for three other words.
10. Ask students to pair off and share their words and examples with their partners.
11. Share the words and examples as a class.
12. Gather all of the students' index cards. Punch a hole in the upper left-hand corner of each card. Place all of the cards on a book ring to create an activity that students can use to reinforce their understanding of different words in a multiple-meaning center.
13. Show students how the center works: one student shows the word to a partner, and the partner tries to think of sentences using the word in different ways.

## EXTRA! EXTRA!

Have students look through their newspapers and cut out sentences that use high-frequency words in different ways. Ask them to glue the examples next to the appropriate words on your word wall.

# Reading Comprehension

**CHAPTER 5**

I have a problem with the movement in many schools to stress phonics in various scripted reading programs. My problem is this: phonics is only one part of reading. Plenty of kids can decode what they are reading. I am willing to bet you can decode the antipiracy warning in French on DVDs. Decoding and comprehending are two vastly different concepts, and each is important. To assist students in understanding what they read, it is a good idea to provide them with reading materials that are of interest to them. Once again, newspapers trump just about any other resource I know.

Newspapers are the Wal-Marts of reading materials: they offer something for everybody.

It is much easier to comprehend what you read when you already have some knowledge about a subject. When I lived in Madrid and struggled with speaking and understanding Spanish, I made sure I put myself in situations where I felt comfortable. While I would have loved to have dined at the classiest restaurants and discussed the meaning of life with Castilian aristocrats, I opted instead to frequent McDonald's and watch Spanish-dubbed versions of American television shows.

Your students will quickly be drawn to newspaper items that let them exhibit their prior knowledge. Many boys follow their favorite sports teams, and they gravitate to the sports section to share their knowledge and opinions of athletes, coaches, and games. Children who enjoy a particular television program take a greater interest in critics' reviews of that show. Although students do not have to be interested in a subject to comprehend it, interest certainly aids their comprehension.

As part of most states' English/language-arts standards for grades 1–3, students are expected to read and understand grade-level-appropriate material. Reading newspapers gives students a chance to use a variety of comprehension strategies. The following mini-lessons are designed to enhance reading comprehension by providing reading materials—which just happen to be newspapers—that appeal to students' interests.

## Acknowledge Experts

One of your most important jobs as an educator is to acknowledge how special your students are each and every day. Find something that each of your students is good at (e.g., Cynthia is good at solving the word jumbles in the newspaper; Paco draws excellent comic strips; Sergio can recite basketball statistics) and refer classmates to that student. I always tried to announce an area of expertise of each of at least five different students every day. You would be surprised how motivated a boy becomes to read the list of famous birthdays in the newspaper if he knows you are going to ask him about it in front of the class. Build these positive experiences into your class day.

# Weather Bingo

**H**ere is a piece of wisdom I have learned: if all else fails, create a bingo game. Students love games like this one, which is also a great way to reinforce their understanding of where they can find specific kinds of information. Despite the title, you do not need to limit yourself to weather bingo. I enjoyed using the weather page because it allowed me to assess my students' learning in a variety of content areas. But feel free to adapt this concept to your favorite section of the newspaper or to any section preferred by your students.

## WHAT YOU NEED

### FOR EACH STUDENT

- **reproducible**
- **newspaper**
- **pencil**

## OBJECTIVE

Students will demonstrate comprehension by identifying answers in the text.

## PROCEDURE

1. Before class, review the reproducible and make sure that the answers to all of the questions can be found in the newspaper you're using. If you find any questions that don't apply, replace them with some of your own. Then make copies of the reproducible.

2. In class, give each student a newspaper and a copy of the reproducible. Make sure everyone has a pencil.

3. Ask students to turn to the section of the newspaper that contains the weather information.

4. Review with students the instructions on the reproducible.

5. Turn 'em loose to play the game!

6. When all of the students have answered all of the questions, review the answers as a class.

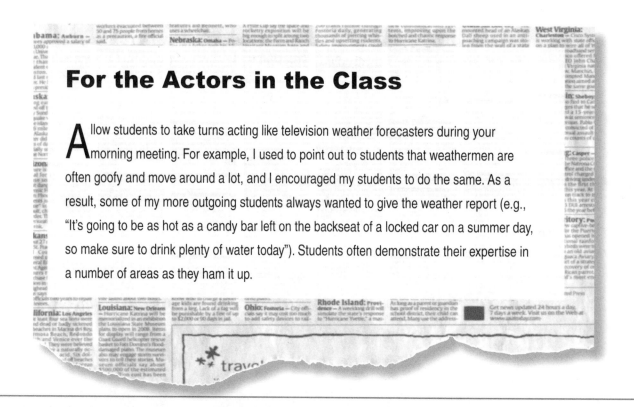

## For the Actors in the Class

**A**llow students to take turns acting like television weather forecasters during your morning meeting. For example, I used to point out to students that weathermen are often goofy and move around a lot, and I encouraged my students to do the same. As a result, some of my more outgoing students always wanted to give the weather report (e.g., "It's going to be as hot as a candy bar left on the backseat of a locked car on a summer day, so make sure to drink plenty of water today"). Students often demonstrate their expertise in a number of areas as they ham it up.

# WEATHER BINGO

Directions: Look through the weather section of your newspaper to find the items below. Circle the answers in the newspaper as you find them. In each blank space, write either the answer or the page number where you can find the answer. When you get four in the same row (vertically, horizontally, or diagonally), stand up and yell, "Bingo!"

| | | | |
|---|---|---|---|
| The high temperature tomorrow will be _____. | Today's sunrise was at _____. | The low temperature for tonight will be _____. | The record low for this date is _____. |
| Write down the title of a story that describes weather conditions. _____ _____. | The weather for tomorrow will be _____ _____. | The air quality for today will be _____ _____. | What city had the same high temperature as our city yesterday? _____ |
| The record high for this date is _____. | Where can you find an outdoor photo taken in our city yesterday? _____ | The normal high for this date is _____. | Where was the hottest temperature in the U.S. recorded yesterday? _____ |
| Winds today will be _____ _____. | Today's sunset will be at _____. | In what year was the record low for this date recorded? _____ | The average low for this date is _____. |

# Cause & Effect Comics

I've read that people who read the comics first live longer than people who read news stories first. If it's not true, it should be. Students love comics because they are funny, and this activity shows students that comics offer a wonderful lesson in concise writing: comics typically try to convey stories in as few frames as possible (usually one to five frames). A comic strip usually shows an action (cause) on the part of one or more characters and a reaction (effect) on the part of one or more other characters. Students enjoy looking at comics and trying to decide what is happening even before they can read the text. This activity also lends itself to a discussion about how every action creates a reaction.

## WHAT YOU NEED

### FOR EACH STUDENT

- **reproducible**
- **newspaper**
- **scissors**
- **glue stick**
- **crayons**
- **pencil**

## OBJECTIVE

Students will recognize cause-and-effect relationships in a text.

## PROCEDURE

1. Before class, make copies of the reproducible.
2. Review cause and effect as a class.
3. Ask students to work in pairs.
4. Hand out the newspapers and the copies of the reproducible.
5. Make sure everyone has scissors, a glue stick, crayons, and a pencil.
6. Explain that each student (not each pair) should cut out a comic strip and glue it in the wide box at the top of the reproducible.
7. Ask each pair to discuss what is happening in each of their comics, looking especially for the cause and effect.
8. Explain that each student should begin his own comic strip. Have him draw a character doing something (the cause) in the left-hand frame of the first pair of cause-and-effect boxes.
9. Ask students to trade papers with their partners. Now tell each student to complete his partner's comic by drawing a reaction (the effect) in the appropriate box.
10. Tell students to discuss the cause and effect in each of their comics.
11. Ask them to practice drawing another two-frame comic together in the second pair of boxes, following the same routine as before.
12. When all of the comics have been completed, ask for volunteers to share their creations with the class.

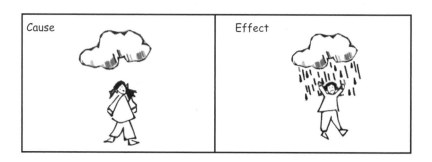

# Cause & Effect Comics

Glue the comic here.

| Cause | Effect |
|---|---|
| | |

| Cause | Effect |
|---|---|
| | |

# The Inverted Pyramid

**N**ewspapers typically try to convey as much information as possible in a limited space. In a similar vein, students enjoy competing with one another to relate as much information as they can with the fewest possible words.

## WHAT YOU NEED

### FOR EACH STUDENT

- **reproducible**
- **newspaper**
- **scissors**
- **glue stick**
- **pencil**
- **paper**

## OBJECTIVE

Students will respond to who, what, when, where, why, and how questions.

## PROCEDURE

1. Before class, make copies of the reproducible.

2. In class, remind students that news stories follow the inverted pyramid style, in which the most important information is presented at the beginning of the story, in the lead.

3. Show students examples of news stories in the newspaper and point out the structure of each story.

4. Explain that a good lead answers who, what, when, where, why, and how.

5. Point out to students that news stories appear throughout the newspaper, not just in the front section.

6. Give a newspaper and a copy of the reproducible to each student.

7. Make sure everyone has scissors, a glue stick, a pencil, and paper.

8. Ask each student to complete the reproducible independently.

9. When everyone has finished, ask the class to brainstorm events that have happened in school during the past week. Write students' ideas on the board.

10. Ask each student to write a lead to a news story describing one of the events the class has brainstormed.

11. Instruct each student to find a partner. Have the partners read their news leads aloud to each other.

12. Ask volunteers to share their news leads with the class.

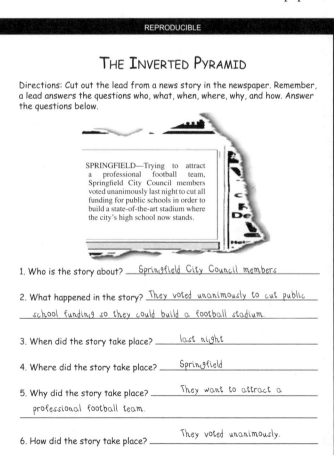

**REPRODUCIBLE**

### THE INVERTED PYRAMID

Directions: Cut out the lead from a news story in the newspaper. Remember, a lead answers the questions who, what, when, where, why, and how. Answer the questions below.

SPRINGFIELD—Trying to attract a professional football team, Springfield City Council members voted unanimously last night to cut all funding for public schools in order to build a state-of-the-art stadium where the city's high school now stands.

1. Who is the story about? _Springfield City Council members_

2. What happened in the story? _They voted unanimously to cut public school funding so they could build a football stadium._

3. When did the story take place? _last night_

4. Where did the story take place? _Springfield_

5. Why did the story take place? _They want to attract a professional football team._

6. How did the story take place? _They voted unanimously._

# THE INVERTED PYRAMID

Directions: Cut out the lead from a news story in the newspaper. Remember, a lead answers the questions who, what, when, where, why, and how. Answer the questions below.

Glue the news story lead here.

1. Who is the story about? _____

2. What happened in the story? _____

_____

3. When did the story take place? _____

4. Where did the story take place? _____

5. Why did the story take place? _____

_____

6. How did the story take place? _____

_____

_____

# Headless Headlines

**S**tudents enjoy trying to match headlines with stories. This is a great matching exercise that can enhance students' predicting skills, allow them to demonstrate how well they comprehend what they read, and motivate them to create their own stimulating stories with appropriate titles.

## WHAT YOU NEED

### FOR EACH STUDENT

- **reproducible**
- **newspaper**
- **scissors**
- **pencil**
- **glue stick**
- **10 sheets of construction paper**
- **manila envelope**

## OBJECTIVE

Students will distinguish the main idea in expository text.

## PROCEDURE

1. Before class, make copies of the reproducible.
2. In class, remind students that headlines in newspapers function as titles of stories and that they often give clues to what the stories are about.
3. Hand out all of the materials.
4. Ask each student to cut out five news stories and their headlines from different sections of the newspaper.
5. Tell students to copy each headline below a different number on the reproducible.
6. Ask them to cut apart the stories and headlines they cut from the newspaper and glue each headline on a separate sheet of construction paper.
7. Add that each student should then turn over each sheet of construction paper and write the appropriate headline number on the back. She should make sure the number on the construction paper matches the number for that headline on the reproducible.
8. Ask students to glue the stories that go with the headlines on separate sheets of construction paper and to write the appropriate numbers from their reproducibles on the backs of those sheets as well.
9. Have each student place her ten sheets of construction paper and one reproducible in a manila envelope.
10. Explain that as each student completes the activity, she should find a partner and trade envelopes with the partner.
11. Ask the pairs to see if they can match each other's headlines with the correct stories.
12. Review the story-headline combinations as a class.
13. Remind students that although headlines function as titles of stories, a headline does not always reveal the story's main idea. Ask students to discuss whether each of the headlines they've chosen conveys the main idea of the story. Challenge them to come up with an alternative for any headline that doesn't tell the main idea.
14. Place the manila envelopes in a center where students can practice matching headlines and stories. This will reinforce their understanding of the main ideas in newspaper articles.

# HEADLESS HEADLINES

Headline #1

_____

_____

Headline #2

_____

_____

Headline #3

_____

_____

Headline #4

_____

_____

Headline #5

_____

_____

# One Step at a Time

This is a good exercise to reinforce clarity in reading and writing directions. Practice like this helps students to realize that what seems clear to them may not be clear to others. Once your students have tried it, you may find them writing lots of cookbooks and how-to manuals for your class library.

## WHAT YOU NEED

### FOR EACH STUDENT

- **reproducible**
- **newspaper**
- **pencil**
- **crayons**
- **paper**

## OBJECTIVE

Students will follow simple multiple-step instructions (e.g., how to assemble a product or play a board game).

## PROCEDURE

1. Before class, make copies of the reproducible.

2. In class, tell students that they can use newspapers to practice following directions (e.g., read recipes, learn how to contact organizations, respond to classified ads). Add that they can also use newspapers to create their own games for following instructions.

3. Hand out all of the materials.

4. Explain to students that they will be writing directions and reading them to a partner; the partner will draw based on the instructions he receives.

5. Tell each student to choose an item that's listed for sale in the classified section of the newspaper and to draw a picture of that item in the box at the top of the reproducible.

6. Tell the student to write the name of the item underneath the picture.

7. Ask each student to write step-by-step instructions explaining how to draw the chosen item. Add that he can continue on the back of the reproducible if he runs out of space. Remind him that he will need to be careful not to give away the name of the item he's chosen.

8. Once all of the students have written their instructions, ask each student to find a partner.

9. Explain that one student in each pair is to read his directions to his partner one step at a time. The partner should follow the directions, then try to guess what the item is.

10. Explain that if the partner correctly guesses the item, the instructions are clear. If not, the two students should discuss how to write better instructions. Then, as a pair, they can rewrite the instructions.

11. Have partners trade positions. If Partner A was the one doing the drawing before, he becomes the reader now, and Partner B tries to follow his directions and guess the item.

12. Allow volunteers to read their directions to the class.

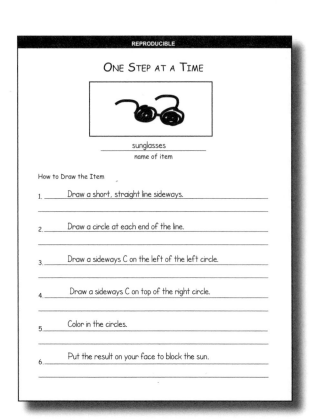

# ONE STEP AT A TIME

_____

name of item

How to Draw the Item


1. _____

_____


2. _____

_____


3. _____

_____


4. _____

_____


5. _____

_____


6. _____

_____

# Graphic Organizer

**M**y students loved *USA Today* because of its colorful diagrams, charts, and graphs (e.g., weather maps, sports statistics, survey results). This is a great way to get students excited about graphing other information, such as attendance, the number of books they've read, and the frequency of parent visits to your classroom. It also lets each student show what he knows in whatever way works best for him.

Note that since this activity requires lots of diagrams, charts, and graphs, it works best with a major metropolitan daily newspaper.

## WHAT YOU NEED

### FOR EACH STUDENT

- scissors
- glue stick
- pencil

### FOR EACH GROUP

- newspaper
- index cards

## OBJECTIVE

Students will interpret information from diagrams, charts, and graphs.

## PROCEDURE

1. Ask students to think about what types of information go into diagrams, charts, and graphs and why newspapers might choose to put information in that format. Discuss this as a class.
2. Ask students to form groups of four or five.
3. Give each group one newspaper and a stack of index cards.
4. Make sure everyone has scissors, a glue stick, and a pencil.
5. Review with students the differences between diagrams, charts, and graphs.
6. Tell students to cut out all of the diagrams, charts, and graphs they can find in the newspaper and glue each one on an individual index card.
7. Instruct students to write the word "diagram," "chart," or "graph" on the back of the card as appropriate.

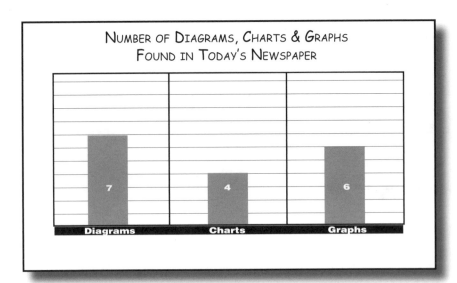

8. Allow the groups to review all of their diagram, chart, and graph cards. Ask them if they can identify what each item is (whether it's a diagram, a chart, or a graph) and interpret what each one says.

9. Invite all of the groups to present the information they have learned to the class. They may deliver their presentations in any way they wish, as long as they convey the information that is in their diagrams, charts, or graphs. They can report the information orally, for example, or they can write a song or create a game.

10. As a class, count the number of different diagrams, graphs, and charts students found. Create a diagram, chart, or graph that records these numbers.

## Post Newspaper Charts

You can motivate your students to read newspapers by posting newspaper charts in your classroom. Keep track of how many students read the newspaper daily, the amount of time they spend reading the newspaper, their favorite sections of the newspaper, and other information that will keep your students thinking about newspapers.

# That Reminds Me

**B**efore we can teach our students, it is imperative that we determine their interests. I constantly shared stories, photos, and ads from the newspaper with my students and asked them if the items reminded them of any stories. This is a great way to get students to connect what they read with their own lives and to use all of their intelligences to express themselves.

## WHAT YOU NEED

### FOR EACH STUDENT

- **reproducible**
- **newspaper**
- **yellow crayon**
- **pencil**

## OBJECTIVE

Students will relate prior knowledge to textual information.

## PROCEDURE

1. Before class, make copies of the reproducible.
2. In class, hand out the newspapers and encourage students to scan all of the sections, looking particularly for information on subjects they're especially interested in.
3. Make sure everyone has a yellow crayon and a pencil.
4. Ask students to highlight with the crayon any items that interest them. These can be stories, photos, ads, or anything else.
5. Ask students why certain stories interest them. Explain that most people prefer reading about subjects that they understand or have an interest in.
6. Give each student a copy of the reproducible.
7. Ask each student to look again at the items she's highlighted. Explain that she should choose from her highlighted pieces just three things that she can relate to her own prior knowledge. Give examples. Students might be able to relate to a comic showing a boy who has broken a lamp, a photo of a woman splashing in a puddle, a sports story about a baseball team losing in the ninth inning, or a classified ad about a truck for sale.
8. Explain that each student should write in the left-hand boxes on the reproducible the section, page number, and headline or description of each story, photo, ad, or other item she has chosen.
9. Ask each student to find a partner.
10. Encourage students to record their personal stories in the right-hand boxes of the reproducible in whatever way is most comfortable for them. Some may want to draw pictures of their experiences, while others may create songs.

---

**REPRODUCIBLE**

## THAT REMINDS ME

Section: _____ D _____

Page: _____ 6 _____

Story/Photo/Ad/Other:
_ad for used truck_

That reminds me of
_when my parents sold our old_
_Honda_

11. Tell each student to share with her partner two to three of the items she chose, along with her explanation of how those items relate to her life. Again, give examples (e.g., "There is an ad for a truck for sale in the classified section, and that reminds me of when my parents sold our old Honda").

12. Ask student volunteers to share their partners' stories. Explain that each volunteer should choose one newspaper item that her partner chose and tell how it relates to her partner's life. Again, each volunteer can convey the story in whatever way she chooses.

## EXTRA! EXTRA!

You can send newspapers home with students and encourage parents to discuss stories that remind them of their own experiences. Get parents in the habit of discussing newspaper content with their children and comparing the parents' and children's reactions to different stories, cartoons, photos, ads, etc. This will provide a model for students. I constantly encouraged my students to share their reactions to newspaper items with me. It was a good way to identify children's interests.

# THAT REMINDS ME

Section: _____

Page: _____

Story/Photo/Ad/Other:

_____

_____

That reminds me of

_____

_____

_____

_____ .

---

Section: _____

Page: _____

Story/Photo/Ad/Other:

_____

_____

That reminds me of

_____

_____

_____

_____ .

---

Section: _____

Page: _____

Story/Photo/Ad/Other:

_____

_____

That reminds me of

_____

_____

_____

_____ .

# CHAPTER 6

# Literary Response & Analysis

Above all, two things made me despise reading as a child: (1) assigned reading and (2) book reports. As a teacher, you can perpetuate routines that you abhor, or you can change the system. I chose to change the system.

Lazy teachers assign reading. Outstanding teachers determine the reading interests of each student. I believe that a teacher can inspire any child to become passionate about seeking knowledge through reading if the teacher provides enough interesting reading materials and discussions about those materials. I have never encountered a student who did not take an interest in newspapers.

True, some of your students will read just the television listings or the comics, and others will enjoy the newspaper only if you read it aloud. I'd like to say that from the moment you distribute newspapers to your first graders, they are going to dive into heated debates about a story in the *Wall Street Journal,* speculating about what the Fed chair is going to do next. I'd like to say that, but that is not the reality. The daily struggles and triumphs of teaching are not those highlighted in movies.

It takes time to improve students' critical analysis of what they read. Anyone who tells you different is a liar, a natural-born teacher, or a space alien. Providing young children with strategies to predict what is going to happen next in their reading, reflect on what has happened so far, and formulate opinions about what they have read is a long, hard process for most teachers. It has been my experience that newspapers make this process much easier and simplify students' transition to analyzing different types of literature.

Many states' English/language-arts standards for grades 1–3 require students to read and respond to a variety of literature. Students need to be able to distinguish different structural features of the text and also to identify specific literary terms or elements (e.g., theme, plot, setting, characters). The following mini-lessons allow students to respond to and analyze different items in newspapers. The goal is to enable your students to use these skills when they encounter other types of writing, particularly significant works of children's literature.

## Encourage Newspaper Buddies

Start the day off right by encouraging each student to talk about his favorite newspaper items of the day with a newspaper buddy while you perform administrative duties such as taking attendance, speaking with parents, and checking homework.

# Weather Haiku

To become better writers, students need to see a variety of writing styles. When you encourage students to use newspapers as a starting point for experimenting with writing different forms of poetry, you get them excited about writing. This activity is a particularly good fit for your naturalist students, because haiku typically deal with nature.

Note that since this strategy relies on newspaper weather pages, it works best with a metropolitan daily newspaper or *USA Today*.

## WHAT YOU NEED

### FOR EACH STUDENT

- **reproducible**
- **newspaper**
- **scissors**
- **glue stick**
- **pencil**

## OBJECTIVE

Students will use poetry in their writing.

## PROCEDURE

1. Before class, make copies of the reproducible.

2. In class, introduce your students to the Japanese form of poetry known as haiku. Explain that a haiku typically records an impression of nature and that it always consists of only three lines. It focuses on the seasons, contrasts, and surprises. Add that the pattern of a haiku is five syllables in the first line, seven syllables in the second line, and five syllables in the third line.

3. Give each student a copy of the reproducible.

4. As a class, review the example given on the reproducible.

5. Also as a class, create a haiku about a hot day during summer vacation.

6. Hand out the newspapers.

7. Make sure everyone has scissors, a glue stick, and a pencil.

8. Ask students to find the weather page in the newspaper.

9. Explain that each student should cut out the weather forecast and glue it in the box on the reproducible.

10. Explain that each student should then go to the bottom of the reproducible and write a haiku about the weather forecast.

11. Ask students to share their weather haiku orally with the rest of the class.

## EXTRA! EXTRA!

As a variation on this activity, try taking students outside and asking them to observe what they find there. Then come back inside and ask each student to create a haiku about what she has seen.

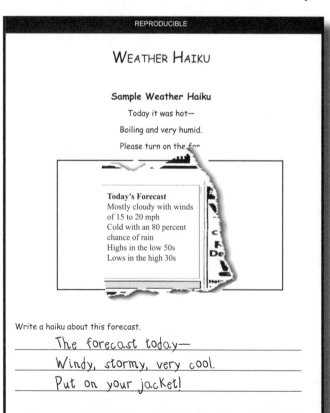

REPRODUCIBLE

WEATHER HAIKU

**Sample Weather Haiku**

Today it was hot—
Boiling and very humid.
Please turn on the fan.

**Today's Forecast**
Mostly cloudy with winds of 15 to 20 mph
Cold with an 80 percent chance of rain
Highs in the low 50s
Lows in the high 30s

Write a haiku about this forecast.

The forecast today—
Windy, stormy, very cool.
Put on your jacket!

# WEATHER HAIKU

## Sample Weather Haiku

Today it was hot—

Boiling and very humid.

Please turn on the fan.

---

Glue the weather forecast here.

---

Write a haiku about this forecast.

_____

_____

_____

# Same Story, Different Views

Young students love to "tattle" on one another. It was one of my biggest pet peeves as a teacher. This is a great activity because it teaches students to look at every situation from multiple points of view.

## WHAT YOU NEED

### FOR EACH STUDENT

- **newspaper**
- **pencil**

### FOR EACH PAIR

- **reproducible**

## OBJECTIVE

Students will compare and contrast different versions of the same stories.

## PROCEDURE

1. Before class, make copies of the reproducible.
2. In class, point out to students that newspapers are filled with opinion. Columnists often interpret news stories from their own points of view. Sometimes the newspapers themselves are biased (e.g., they promote or put down certain events, people, or causes). Show specific examples.
3. Hand out the newspapers and encourage students to scan them for examples of writing that incorporates opinion.
4. Using the examples in the illustration if you like, model for students how the same information can be conveyed from different points of view.
5. Ask students to form pairs.
6. Give each pair a copy of the reproducible.
7. Make sure everyone has a pencil.
8. Instruct each pair to find headlines or captions from three different sections of the newspaper.
9. Ask each pair to copy the headlines or captions in the first row of boxes on the reproducible.

10. Explain that one partner is to rewrite each headline or caption from one point of view and the other partner is to rewrite the headline or caption from a different point of view.
11. Have students record their work in the second and third boxes of the reproducible.
12. Ask students if they see a bias in each newspaper headline or caption.

## EXTRA! EXTRA!

Ask students to create their own newspapers written from specific points of view. For example, they could create a newspaper edited by the Big Bad Wolf and write stories that make the Three Little Pigs look like they deserve to have their houses blown down.

---

REPRODUCIBLE

SAME STORY, DIFFERENT VIEWS

| Headline/Caption | Midvale 14, Springfield 0<br><br>Tomorrow's Forecast: Partly Cloudy with 80 Percent Chance of Rain, High in the Low 60s<br><br>Janet Mason Signs Movie Contract for $5 Million |
| --- | --- |
| One Point of View | Midvale Destroys Springfield<br><br>Showers Expected to Put Damper on Tomorrow<br><br>Spoiled Prima Donna Inks Record-Breaking Movie Deal |
| Different Point of View | Springfield Loses a Heartbreaker<br><br>Much-Needed Rain Likely<br><br>Starlet Receives Well-Deserved Raise |

# SAME STORY, DIFFERENT VIEWS

| Headline/Caption | |
| :---: | --- |
| **One Point of View** | |
| **Different Point of View** | |

# Subliminal Messages

**S**tudents enjoy scanning newspapers to determine how they portray various people. This is a good opportunity to point out how words and pictures can influence readers in ways that aren't always obvious.

## WHAT YOU NEED

### FOR EACH STUDENT

- **newspaper**
- **scissors**
- **glue stick**
- **2 sheets of construction paper**
- **2 pieces of yarn**

### FOR EACH GROUP

- **2 clothes hangers**
- **hole punch**

## OBJECTIVE

Students will determine how the author or illustrator portrays individual characters.

## PROCEDURE

1.  Tell students that items in various parts of the newspaper try to persuade readers to think in certain ways.
2.  Point out that many photographs in newspapers tend to make people look very smart or very silly, advertisements try to sell products by convincing people they need certain items, and writers may express their own opinions in news stories by focusing on specific characteristics.
3.  Remind students that although the editorial page is filled with opinion, many other parts of the newspaper include opinion, too. From movie reviews to sports columns, many elements of the newspaper are intended to influence the way people think.
4.  Ask students to work in groups of four or five.
5.  Hand out the newspapers.
6.  Make sure everyone has scissors, a glue stick, and two sheets of construction paper.
7.  Ask everyone to scan the newspaper for articles, advertisements, photos, and cartoons that portray people in positive and negative ways. Remind students that editorial cartoons often portray people in negative ways by exaggerating certain personal features (e.g., an athlete's muscular body or a political candidate's facial features), making the subject look silly.
8.  Explain that each student should cut out both silly and serious characters and glue them on separate sheets of construction paper—silly on one, serious on the other.
9.  Give each student two pieces of yarn. Give each group two clothes hangers and a hole punch.
10. Direct students to punch a hole in the top of each sheet of construction paper. Explain that the students in each group should use the yarn to tie all of their silly characters to one clothes hanger and all of their serious characters to another.
11. Allow each group to present their clothes hanger collages to the class and explain why they classified their characters as either silly or serious.
12. Hang the collages in the classroom so they can be used as a center. You can place the collages in a closet or clothes hanger center (see page 46) or hang them from the classroom ceiling. The latter is particularly easy for teachers whose classrooms have ceilings with individual, removable panels.

# The Sounds of the Newspaper

**S**tudents love to hear the sounds of the newspaper. Use those sounds to engage them in this lesson in alliteration and onomatopoeia. Don't be afraid to ham it up as you add the sound effects to your reading!

## WHAT YOU NEED

### FOR EACH STUDENT

- **newspaper**
- **scissors**
- **glue stick**
- **paper**
- **pencil**

### FOR THE TEACHER

- **marker**
- **butcher paper**

## OBJECTIVE

Students will recognize the similarities of sounds in words and rhythmic patterns (e.g., alliteration, onomatopoeia) in a selection.

## PROCEDURE

1. Review alliteration and onomatopoeia with students.
2. Read aloud stories from the newspaper. Bring your read-aloud to life by adding sound effects. For example, if you read an article about a NASCAR race, make the sounds of racecars, brakes, crowd noise, etc.
3. Point out that headlines and photo captions in newspapers often feature alliteration and onomatopoeia.
4. As a class, brainstorm examples of onomatopoeia (e.g., wham, clip-clop, vroom). List students' suggestions on a sheet of butcher paper.
5. As a class, create some headlines that feature alliteration. You may want to come up with examples for different sections of the newspaper. A headline for the classifieds could read "Try a Terrific Toyota Truck." For sports, the class might write, "Trojans Trounce Tigers." For weather, you might write something like "Blizzard Buries Boston."
6. Hand out all of the materials.
7. Ask each student to choose a picture from anywhere in the newspaper, cut it out, and glue it at the top of a sheet of paper.

Bang! Bambino blasts bomb!

8. Explain that each student may choose between creating an advertisement or writing a caption for her picture, but she must use both alliteration and onomatopoeia.
9. Instruct each student to write her advertisement or caption below the picture.
10. Ask for volunteers to share their work with the class.

# Three Strikes

Students—especially aspiring sleuths—love this activity. It's a great way to get students to pay attention to details and work on their questioning skills. In addition, you get a chance to see how familiar students have become with newspaper language and with the sections of a newspaper.

## WHAT YOU NEED

### FOR EACH STUDENT

- **newspaper**
- **paper**
- **scissors**
- **glue stick**
- **pencil**

### FOR THE TEACHER

- **marker**
- **manila envelope**

## OBJECTIVE

Students will identify the speaker or narrator in a selection and identify different sections of a newspaper (e.g., editorials, obituaries, front-page news stories).

## PROCEDURE

1. Ask students if they have favorite newspaper writers or sections.

2. Read aloud stories from different writers and different sections. See if students can figure out who wrote a particular story and can identify the types of writing (e.g., editorials, obituaries, front-page news stories) that appear in different sections.

3. Select a story from any section of the newspaper.

4. Do not read the story aloud. Tell students you want them to guess which part of the newspaper you are looking at. Tell students they may ask as many questions as they'd like as a class, but they get only three guesses. Call this game Three Strikes.

5. Give students clues about the story.

6. Each time a student guesses incorrectly, write an X on the board.

7. Continue until students get three strikes or someone guesses correctly, whichever comes first.

8. Give each student a newspaper and a sheet of paper.

9. Make sure everyone has scissors, a glue stick, and a pencil.

10. Explain that each student should scan her newspaper and cut out an item that she would like to use for Three Strikes.

11. Add that she should glue the item on one side of her paper. On the back of the paper, she should write at least five clues to the section of the newspaper that her item comes from.

12. Allow several students to read their clues in front of the class. Following the same procedure as before, see if the class can correctly identify the section each item comes from.

13. Place the students' papers in a manila envelope marked "Three Strikes" for use in a center. Students can play the Three Strikes game in pairs, with one student giving the clues and the other asking questions and guessing which section of the newspaper the item appeared in.

# T. Fortwo, 93, Founded the Giving Tree

*Philanthropist T. Fortwo donated millions to various local charities. He died at home on Friday at age 93.*

SEATTLE (AB)—Billionaire T. Fortwo, one of the world's wealthiest men, passed away Friday evening after a long bout with leukemia. He was 93.

Surrounded by friends and family, Fortwo's last wish was that all of his money be given to Seattle's much-troubled and beleaguered school district.

"He was a great man," said Mo Forme, the president of the Take Rich Folks' Money Foundation. "We will sorely miss him."

Fortwo had given millions to different charities before focusing specifically on education. He credited education for making him all of his money and providing him with the moral foundation not to mess up society.

## Clues

1.   I appear in the newspaper every day.

2.   You may feel sad after reading me.

3.   You will appear in this section of the newspaper someday.

4.   Athletes, actors, businesspeople, and other people all appear in this section of the newspaper.

5.   This part of the newspaper is deadly.

# Rewrite the Ending

**S**tudents adore coming up with alternative scenarios. Note that this does not have to be a writing activity. If you prefer, allow your students to share alternative story endings with one another orally. Or let them act out stories with puppets and perform different endings of their skits.

## WHAT YOU NEED

### FOR EACH STUDENT

- **reproducible**
- **newspaper**
- **scissors**
- **glue stick**
- **pencil**

## OBJECTIVE

Students will generate alternative endings to plots.

## PROCEDURE

1. Before class, make copies of the reproducible.
2. In class, point out that newspapers often feature a lot of sad stories.
3. Hand out the newspapers and challenge students to scan them for stories with sad endings.
4. As a class, try changing the sad endings to happier ones.
5. Ask each student to work with a partner.
6. Give a copy of the reproducible to each student.
7. Make sure everyone has scissors, a glue stick, and a pencil.
8. Explain that each student should complete the reproducible independently by finding a newspaper story with a sad ending, cutting out the story and gluing it in the box, and then writing a happy ending to the story.
9. Once the reproducibles have been completed, ask the pairs to share their sad and happy endings with each other. See if the partners can think of alternative happy endings.
10. Ask for volunteers to share their alternative endings with the class.

## Build Community Awareness

**E**ncourage your students to pay attention to upcoming community events. Point out all of the free activities your community offers (e.g., concerts in the park, safety seminars, fun runs), and build students' interest in participating either with their families or with you and their classmates. My students used to claim that they had nothing to do on the weekends because they did not have much money. I showed them that newspapers routinely print announcements for a variety of free activities going on in the community.

# REWRITE THE ENDING

Glue the newspaper story with a sad ending here.

## Happy Ending

_____

_____

_____

_____

_____

_____

# What's It All About?

**T**his activity uses one of students' favorite parts of the newspaper, the comics, to get them to pay attention to plot, setting, and character(s). Students enjoy creating their own comics and thinking of alternative plots, settings, and characters for existing comics (e.g., what if Charlie Brown were a girl and Snoopy were a cat).

## WHAT YOU NEED

### FOR EACH STUDENT

- **reproducible**
- **newspaper**
- **pencil**
- **crayons**

## OBJECTIVE

Students will identify and describe the elements of plot, setting, and character(s) in a story, as well as the story's beginning, middle, and end.

## PROCEDURE

1. Before class, make copies of the reproducible.

2. In class, review plot, setting, and character(s) with students.

3. Point out that comic strips do a great job of telling stories with only a few pictures and words.

4. Hand out the newspapers and ask students to read several comic strips.

5. As a class, discuss which comic strips do the best jobs of telling a complete story with a clear beginning, middle, and end. Ask students how important good characters are to comic strips and what role setting plays in them. For instance, ask if *Peanuts* would be interesting without Charlie Brown and Snoopy, or why people who work in offices like *Dilbert*.

6. Ask each student to find a partner.

7. Give each student a copy of the reproducible.

8. Make sure everyone has a pencil and crayons.

9. Instruct each student to draw a comic strip in the boxes on the reproducible. Note that she should be sure her comic has a clear beginning, middle, and end and that it shows the characters and setting clearly.

10. Tell each student to show her comic strip to her partner.

11. Then tell each student to answer all of the questions on her partner's reproducible. Explain that if she can answer all of the questions, her partner has drawn a good cartoon.

12. Ask for volunteers to share their cartoons with the class.

13. Post all of your students' comic strips around the classroom and have students vote on their favorites. This allows students to see their classmates' work and compare it with their own.

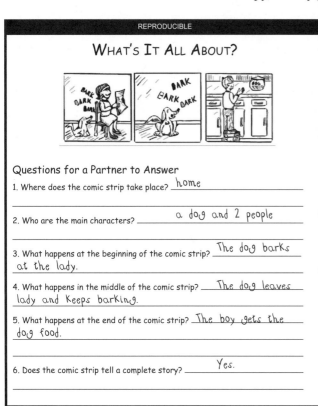

REPRODUCIBLE

### WHAT'S IT ALL ABOUT?

Questions for a Partner to Answer

1. Where does the comic strip take place? home

2. Who are the main characters? a dog and 2 people

3. What happens at the beginning of the comic strip? The dog barks at the lady.

4. What happens in the middle of the comic strip? The dog leaves lady and keeps barking.

5. What happens at the end of the comic strip? The boy gets the dog food.

6. Does the comic strip tell a complete story? Yes.

14. Reward your top cartoonists by allowing them to illustrate class big books, create illustrations for posters, and do other drawing projects.

## EXTRA! EXTRA!

Some comics have only one panel. Allow students to find one of these cartoons in the newspaper and create alternative characters, settings, or plots (or all three). To accommodate all of the students' interests and comfort levels, allow each student to draw her new story, act it out, record it on a tape recorder, or communicate it through whatever other approach she feels comfortable using.

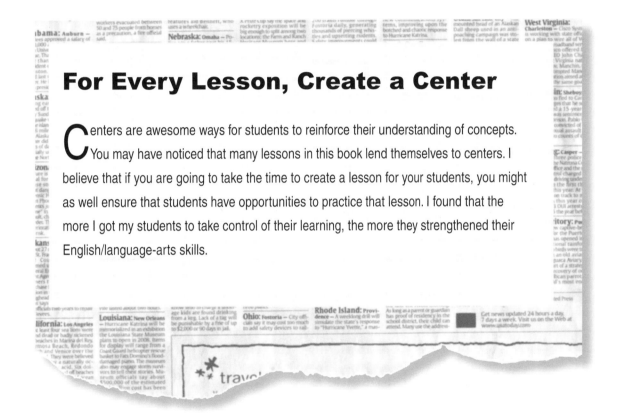

# For Every Lesson, Create a Center

Centers are awesome ways for students to reinforce their understanding of concepts. You may have noticed that many lessons in this book lend themselves to centers. I believe that if you are going to take the time to create a lesson for your students, you might as well ensure that students have opportunities to practice that lesson. I found that the more I got my students to take control of their learning, the more they strengthened their English/language-arts skills.

# WHAT'S IT ALL ABOUT?

| | | |
|---|---|---|
| | | |
| | | |

## Questions for a Partner to Answer

1. Where does the comic strip take place? _____

_____

2. Who are the main characters? _____

_____

3. What happens at the beginning of the comic strip? _____

_____

4. What happens in the middle of the comic strip? _____

_____

5. What happens at the end of the comic strip? _____

_____

6. Does the comic strip tell a complete story? _____

_____

# CHAPTER 7

# Writing Strategies

Tell students that they are going to write, and often they respond with a chorus of moans. Too many students associate writing with misery because they have to struggle to write. Translation: many students do not write well. But you can use newspapers to introduce students to all sorts of fun writing activities that will make them happier, better writers.

Newspapers include text written for a variety of purposes, and that variety lends itself perfectly to teaching. While many students dread writing essays, they may enjoy writing the cutlines, or captions, for photographs. Encouraging students to write classified ads or comic strips can help them to recognize that writing does not always have to feel like work. I found that third graders who dreaded writing stories could be motivated to write angry letters to the editor. Again, newspapers offer a wide range of possibilities for inspiring potential writers.

Many states' English/language-arts standards for grades 1–3 require students to be able to write clear and coherent sentences and paragraphs that develop a central idea. Students' writing must demonstrate that they have considered the audience for and purpose of their writing. Additionally, students typically are expected to progress through the stages of the writing process (prewriting, drafting, revising, editing, publishing). The following mini-lessons are intended to build students' interest in writing through the use of newspapers.

## Provide Newspapers—and Provide Time to Read Them

If I can encourage you to do one thing every day in your classroom, it is to allow your students some time to read their newspapers for fun. I sound like Sally Struthers, but if you would give your students just ten minutes a day—the time it takes to drink a cup of coffee—you could significantly impact their reading habits for a lifetime.

# Cut to the Chase

I found that when I asked students to describe pictures, they responded in one of three ways: some shrugged their shoulders and said, "I don't know"; some described every detail of the picture for eight minutes and added several random personal anecdotes; and some described specific features when prompted. We want students to respond more consistently and appropriately. Here's a way to get them there.

## WHAT YOU NEED

### FOR EACH STUDENT

- **newspaper**
- **4 large index cards**
- **scissors**
- **glue stick**
- **pencil**

### FOR EVERY 8 STUDENTS

- **manila envelope**

### FOR THE TEACHER

- **photograph**

## OBJECTIVE

Students will use clear and specific vocabulary to communicate ideas.

## PROCEDURE

1. Hand out the newspapers.
2. Read aloud some of the cutlines (captions) that appear below photos in the newspaper.
3. Ask students to scan their own newspapers, looking for photos with cutlines.
4. Tell students that although "a picture is worth a thousand words," the cutline that accompanies a photo can contain only a limited number of words with which to convey the main idea.
5. Show the class a photo from a newspaper or any other source. Ask students to describe the photo aloud in a way that will attract a reader's attention while using as few words as possible. Remind students that cutlines usually capture the main idea of a story.
6. Ask each student to find a partner.
7. Hand out the index cards.
8. Make sure everyone has scissors, a glue stick, and a pencil.
9. Explain that each pair of students should look at photos throughout the newspaper, choose four, and cut them out.
10. Ask each pair to glue each photo on an index card.
11. Tell them to take their remaining index cards and write an original cutline for each photo on a separate card.
12. Ask each pair of students to share their index cards with another pair to see if the other students can match the photos with their cutlines.
13. After all of the students have completed this task, take the cards from four pairs and place them in a manila envelope. Repeat with the cards from the other pairs. (For a class of thirty-two students, you would need four envelopes.) These envelopes can function as a matching center, allowing students to practice this activity during free-choice time or when they complete other activities early.

# All About Me

**S**tudents enjoy using newspapers as a springboard for creating different forms of writing. One of those forms is poetry. Incorporating poetry into your lessons can be a great way to motivate students to read and write, as poems are typically much more succinct than stories. This activity encourages students to write acrostic poems by searching for adjectives in newspaper headlines and advertisements.

## WHAT YOU NEED

### FOR EACH STUDENT

- **paper**
- **pencil**
- **scissors**
- **glue stick**
- **newspaper**

A wesome
N ice
G reat
E fficient
L ovely
A mazing

## OBJECTIVE

Students will use descriptive words when writing.

## PROCEDURE

1. Tell students that poetry is one form of literature that can take many shapes. Explain that an acrostic is a poem in which each letter of a word (usually a person's name) becomes the first letter of an adjective used to describe the person, place, or thing being named.

2. Show students examples of acrostics. For example, write the first name of a famous actor or athlete on the board. As a class, brainstorm adjectives that start with the letters of the person's name and that describe him.

3. As a class, create an acrostic from the words "our class."

4. Make sure everyone has paper, a pencil, scissors, and a glue stick.

5. Ask each student to write her first name vertically on a sheet of paper.

6. Hand out the newspapers. Tell students to scan their newspapers for adjectives that describe them. Advise students to look in headlines and large-print advertisements to find adjectives that begin with the letters of their first names.

7. Tell them to cut out the adjectives and glue them on their papers so that the first letters of the adjectives correctly spell the students' first names.

8. Ask students to share their acrostics orally.

## EXTRA! EXTRA!

Students should be able to find large-print adjectives that describe themselves. If they do not, suggest that they cut out individual letters (ransom-note style) and create adjectives that way.

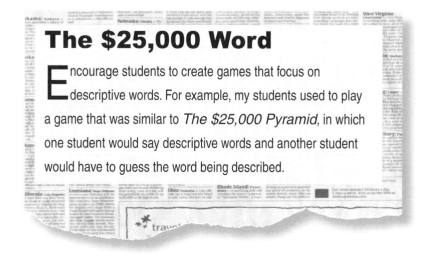

### The $25,000 Word

**E**ncourage students to create games that focus on descriptive words. For example, my students used to play a game that was similar to *The $25,000 Pyramid*, in which one student would say descriptive words and another student would have to guess the word being described.

# Name That Reference!

This is a great way to reinforce the appropriate use of reference materials. Try turning the lesson into a game show, à la *Name That Tune*. And put some energy into it! Your students will get a bigger kick out of the game—and become more engaged—if you "agonize" over presenting a question that you pretend is too difficult for them and then act shocked when they get the answer. Play it up!

You can also appeal to a variety of intelligences with this activity. Encourage your intrapersonal learners to reflect on the different types of information they can find in different reference materials. Allow interpersonal learners to interview intrapersonal learners and present information to the class. Verbal/linguistic, musical/rhythmic, and bodily/kinesthetic learners also may want to present to the class.

## WHAT YOU NEED

### FOR EACH STUDENT

- **reproducible**
- **newspaper**
- **pencil**
- **index cards**

### FOR THE TEACHER

- **marker**
- **manila envelope**

## OBJECTIVE

Students will understand the purposes of various reference materials (dictionary, thesaurus, atlas, encyclopedia).

## PROCEDURE

1. Before class, make copies of the reproducible.
2. In class, review with students the setup and uses of different types of reference materials (e.g., dictionary, thesaurus, atlas, encyclopedia).
3. Hand out the copies of the reproducible and tell students to look over the instructions to get a sense of what they're going to be doing.
4. Hand out the newspapers.
5. Make sure everyone has a pencil.
6. Instruct students to scan the appropriate sections of the newspaper, find the answers to the questions on the reproducible, and fill them in.
7. Review the answers as a class.
8. Hand out the index cards.
9. Ask students to create new reference questions based on something that appeared in a newspaper article. Explain that each question should require other students to use a reference source to find out more about the topic.
10. Have students write each question on an index card, then turn the card over and write the answer on the back of the card.
11. Review students' written questions and answers as a class.
12. Mark a manila envelope "Name That Reference!" and ask students to place their cards in it.
13. Place the envelope in a center and encourage students to use it to reinforce their understanding of appropriate references.

## Answer Key

1. encyclopedia
2. thesaurus
3. dictionary
4. atlas

# NAME THAT REFERENCE!

Directions: Next to each question, write the reference that would best help you to answer the question: atlas, dictionary, encyclopedia, or thesaurus.

1. Look at the obituary page. Which reference book could help you find out more about a person?

_____

2. Look at a headline on the sports page. Which reference book could help you find other words to describe the same thing?

_____

3. Read a front-page news story. Which reference book could help you determine what a new word means?

_____

4. Look at the dateline of a story. Which reference book could help you find that city?

_____

# Funny Paragraphs

Encourage students to have fun with newspapers by cutting out words from headlines and creating their own funny paragraphs. This is a great way to get students thinking about how to connect supporting details to the main idea of a paragraph. It also works well as a way to encourage students with different talents to work together—having one student in a group write the paragraph, for example, and another student read it or act it out. My students asked for this activity constantly.

## WHAT YOU NEED

### FOR EACH STUDENT

- **paper**
- **pencil**
- **crayons**
- **newspaper**
- **scissors**
- **glue stick**

### FOR EACH GROUP

- **poster board**

## OBJECTIVE

Students will group related ideas and maintain a consistent focus. They will create a single paragraph that (1) develops a topic sentence and (2) includes simple supporting facts and details.

## PROCEDURE

1. Show students several different types of newspapers (e.g., local, national, tabloid).
2. Explain to students that the tabloid newspapers they often see at supermarkets present a lot of funny stories that are designed to interest people in buying those newspapers.
3. As a class, review the sample funny paragraph from the illustration.
4. Ask students to form groups of four or five.
5. Make sure everyone has paper, a pencil, and crayons.
6. Ask each group to come up with a funny paragraph. Explain that each student should write the paragraph and draw a corresponding picture on her paper.

---

### Cops Bust Mother for Forcing Children to Eat Vegetables

SPRINGFIELD (AB)—An area woman spent last night in jail after police arrested her for making her children eat their broccoli, a police spokesperson said. Police took Lorna Lesson into custody at 6:30 P.M. last night. Neighbors heard Lesson's children whining and dialed 911. There is no word on what the children might be eating for dinner tonight.

7. Each funny paragraph should have the following elements:

    a. a headline

    b. a topic sentence, or lead

    c. at least three sentences that support the lead

    d. a picture

8. Remind students that a good lead answers the questions who, what, when, where, why, and how. Point out to students that the supporting sentences in each funny paragraph should expand on information given in the lead.

9. Hand out the newspapers. Make sure everyone has scissors and a glue stick.

10. Ask students to cut out words from headlines, captions, and advertisements to create their funny paragraphs. Have each group glue the words on poster board, ransom-note style.

11. Tell each group to cut out a funny picture that goes with their paragraph or to use one of the pictures they drew earlier. Have them glue the picture next to their story.

12. Ask the groups to share their funny paragraphs with the class.

13. Hang the posters on bulletin boards around the classroom.

# Find Time-Savers

Newspapers are filled with abbreviations and symbols. Challenge students to scan their newspapers for time-saving symbols and abbreviations. (For example, weather maps have pictures of the sun to indicate sunny weather, clouds for cloudy weather, etc.) Ask students to create symbols and abbreviations for your classroom. My first graders, for instance, drew pictures to identify different centers.

# Writing Applications

I was blessed to have a lot of very good English/language-arts teachers throughout my childhood. They encouraged me to experiment with different types of writing and constantly hone my skills. As a result, I enjoy writing. When I became a teacher, I wanted to ignite a similar passion for writing in my students. Textbooks did not entice my students, but newspapers sure did.

The best way you can get your students to write more is to give them reasons to write. I do not know any second grader who has much use for an essay, but I know plenty who are interested in knowing how to write letters to companies to request free stuff. Asking students to describe their summer vacations is one way to get them to share personal experiences. Challenging students to write reviews of their favorite new video games, movies, or—heaven forbid—books is a better way.

By getting your students in the habit of reading the newspaper every day, you are presenting them with countless models of good, concise, and varied writing. There are many pieces to every puzzle, and I wanted my students to know that newspapers offer many formats and styles that can be models for exemplary writing. By exposing students to different writing activities that they could pursue based on their newspaper reading, I managed to convince them that writing essays was not such a bad thing.

As part of the English/language-arts standards for grades 1–3 in many states, students are expected to be able to write compositions that describe and explain familiar objects, events, and experiences. Students' writing must display a command of standard American English (academic language) and of the writing process, along with research and organizational skills. The following mini-lessons are designed to show students how to write for different audiences and purposes.

## Develop Student-Interest Files

Whenever your students find an article about a person, place, or thing they admire, encourage them to clip the article and add it to your classroom's file regarding student interests. You can use this file to discuss students' aspirations. Encourage your students to spend time visualizing themselves fulfilling their dreams. For example, if your students want to go to Hawaii, encourage them to clip stories and photos of Hawaii and spend time each day thinking about traveling to Hawaii.

# Thumbs Up/Thumbs Down

This activity encourages students to view items in the newspaper with a more critical eye. Encourage them to have fun with their movie blurbs but to remember that their goal is to convince readers to see the movie.

## WHAT YOU NEED

### FOR EACH STUDENT

- **newspaper**
- **paper**
- **pencil**
- **crayons**

## OBJECTIVE

Students will write brief narratives (e.g., fictional, autobiographical) describing an experience.

## PROCEDURE

1. Tell students that newspapers are filled with opinions about clothes, cars, movies, etc. Point out that many newspaper columnists write about their own experiences in order to inform others.
2. Hand out all of the materials.
3. Tell students to turn to the entertainment section of the newspaper and to scan the movie ads.
4. Invite students to read aloud comments from critics about various movies.
5. Ask each student to come up with an idea for a movie, then create a poster advertising it. Show students the illustration as an example.
6. Have each student draw a scene from the movie on a sheet of paper.
7. Ask each student to write two or three blurbs beneath his picture that will make people want to see the movie. Explain that all of the blurbs need to be written as complete sentences.
8. Discuss the posters as a class, then display them on the classroom walls.

## EXTRA! EXTRA!

Different teachers have different resources available to them. Some teachers have video cameras and allow students to use the cameras to create trailers (previews to entice viewers) for their movies. Some students have their own video cameras and can shoot trailers on their own. Allow students to share these trailers with the class. My students and I did not have video resources, but we had old tape recorders and cheap cassettes. We often used them to tape-record audio movie trailers. This activity is also an opportunity for your "performer" students to play with voice impersonations.

"This is the scariest movie I've seen in years."
—Jim Nasium, Springfield Gazette

"I laughed. I cried. This movie touched me as no other film has before."
—Shirley Uno, ABZ News

"You'll never want to go to school again!"
—Ginger Vitus, Instant Reviews

# Job Search

**S**tudents enjoy looking for jobs that interest them. You can learn a lot about your students from this activity, and they can learn a lot, too. While the reproducible focuses on letter-writing skills, the interview makes this a superb choice for practicing speaking and listening skills as well.

## WHAT YOU NEED

### FOR EACH STUDENT

- **reproducible**
- **newspaper**
- **pencil**
- **paper**

## OBJECTIVE

Students will write personal and formal letters that (1) show awareness of the knowledge and interests of the audience and establish a purpose and context and (2) include the date, proper salutation, body, closing, and signature.

## PROCEDURE

1. Before class, make copies of the reproducible.
2. In class, point out to students that people who are looking for jobs often read the classified section of the newspaper.
3. Hand out the newspapers and show students the job listings in the classified section.
4. Give each student a copy of the reproducible.
5. Make sure everyone has a pencil and paper.
6. Ask each student to search the classifieds for a job that appeals to him.
7. Have each student write a letter applying for that job, following the directions on the reproducible.
8. When everyone has finished writing, ask each student to find a partner and exchange letters with that partner. Explain that each student is to read his partner's letter.
9. Allow partners to role-play a job interview. Tell them to take turns playing the parts of the employer and the applicant.

## EXTRA! EXTRA!

Ask each student to create a list of her five favorite jobs. This will help you to develop a better sense of each student's interests. The jobs do not have to be listed in the classifieds, but you can encourage students to use the classified section of the newspaper as a source of ideas.

---

**REPRODUCIBLE**

### JOB SEARCH

Directions: Scan the classified section of the newspaper and look for jobs in the help wanted ads. Decide on the job you would most like to have. Then write a letter to your potential employer explaining why you would like the job and why you should be hired.

Preferred Job: _____Teacher_____

_____March 14, 2008_____

[Date]

Dear _____Mrs. Knowitall_____:

[Address the employer as Mr., Ms., or Mrs.]

I am the top second grader at Rosa Parks Elementary School.

[In the first sentence, tell the employer a little about yourself.]

I want to be a teacher at your school because I like to help kids.

[In the second sentence, tell the employer why you would like the job.]

You should hire me because I'm a good teacher who cares about kids.

[In the third sentence, tell the employer why you should be hired.]

Please let me meet you so you can see why I would be a good teacher.

[In the fourth sentence, request an interview.]

Respectfully,

_____Marilena_____

[Your signature]

# JOB SEARCH

Directions: Scan the classified section of the newspaper and look for jobs in the help wanted ads. Decide on the job you would most like to have. Then write a letter to your potential employer explaining why you would like the job and why you should be hired.

Preferred Job:_____

_____
[Date]

Dear _____:
[Address the employer as Mr., Ms., or Mrs.]

_____
[In the first sentence, tell the employer a little about yourself.]

_____
[In the second sentence, tell the employer why you would like the job.]

_____
[In the third sentence, tell the employer why you should be hired.]

_____
[In the fourth sentence, request an interview.]

Respectfully,

_____
[Your signature]

# The Guessing Game

H ere's a chance for students to find objects in the newspaper that they can describe to others without naming the objects. Photos in advertisements work especially well for this game, which gives students a chance to have fun and interact with one another while learning to write descriptive sentences.

## WHAT YOU NEED

### FOR EACH STUDENT

- **newspaper**
- **index card**
- **scissors**
- **glue stick**
- **pencil**

### FOR THE TEACHER

- **sample poems**

## OBJECTIVE

Students will write brief expository descriptions of real objects, people, places, or events, using sensory details.

## PROCEDURE

1. Read aloud to your students poems that evoke strong sensory images—that is, that stimulate all five senses.
2. Tell students that they will be writing their own ads to get people to buy their products. Remind students of how the poems you read appealed to their senses.
3. Read aloud the sentences from the illustration one at a time. Ask students if they can guess what the product is.
4. Hand out the newspapers and the index cards.
5. Make sure everyone has scissors, a glue stick, and a pencil.
6. Explain that students should scan the newspaper for advertisements with photos.
7. Tell each student to cut out a photograph of a product and glue it on an index card.
8. Ask each student to write on the opposite side of the index card five sentences that describe the object in the photograph. Remind students to write descriptions that call on all five senses.
9. Ask each student to find a partner.
10. Explain that in each pair of students, Student A should give her partner clues about her object by reading her descriptive sentences one at a time. After each clue, Student B should try to guess the object.
11. Add that when Student A has finished giving her clues, the partners should swap roles and repeat the process with Student B's sentences.
12. Tell students that the winner of the game is the person who can guess the item correctly from the fewest clues.

## EXTRA! EXTRA!

When I toured Mark Twain's house in Hartford, Connecticut, the docent pointed out ten items on the fireplace. He said that every night, Twain's daughters would rearrange the items and ask their father to tell a story that used the items in the new order. That sounded like a great storytelling activity, so I adapted it to create a version my students really enjoyed. To try this in your classroom, ask your students to get into groups of four or five. Explain that they will use the photo cards they created for the guessing game activity to tell stories. Have them arrange the cards in any order, then have one student make up a story incorporating the items on the cards. Explain that next they should rearrange the cards and have another student tell a story. Have them repeat this process until each of the students has had a turn.

## Descriptive Sentences

1. I come in an orange container.

2. My name might remind you of the beach.

3. I feel wet.

4. I smell fresh, but you would not want to taste me.

5. You use me to clean up your act.

# Letter to the Editor

**M**y students loved expressing their viewpoints in the letters to the editor section of our classroom newspaper. As a matter of fact, I urge you to have your students write letters to the editor of your local newspaper. It is a great way for them to practice letter writing. Encourage students to visit the Web site of the newspaper they're reading (see page 137 for a list of Web sites) and to e-mail their letters to the editor. Point out that students should include their ages in the signature along with their names. Students will usually get a response from newspapers, and newspapers will often publish students' letters. To get your students addicted to writing, just let them see their names in print!

This is also a great exercise to show students that different types of letters require different formats (e.g., an E-mail does not require a date; a business letter has a different format and uses different expressions than a personal letter).

## WHAT YOU NEED

### FOR EACH STUDENT

- **reproducible**
- **newspaper**
- **pencil**

## OBJECTIVE

Students will write a friendly letter or thank-you note that (1) shows awareness of the knowledge and interests of the audience and establishes a purpose and context and (2) includes the date, proper salutation, body, closing, and signature.

## PROCEDURE

1. Before class, make copies of the reproducible.
2. As a class, review basic letter format.
3. Hand out the newspapers and draw students' attention to the editorial page.
4. Discuss with students how readers of newspapers express—among other things—their gratitude for and dismay over articles by writing letters to the editor.
5. Make sure everyone has a pencil.
6. Pass out copies of the reproducible and ask students to follow the directions.
7. Ask for volunteers to read their letters aloud to the class.

## Appreciation Time

**A**t the end of each day, I used to allow students to stand and read aloud thank-you notes they had created for their classmates. For example, if Felipe helped Rodrigo with his place-value exercises, Rodrigo might write a thank-you note to Felipe that he would read aloud (or ask another person to read aloud). You can cover a number of English/language-arts objectives with this simple activity, and it teaches your students good manners, as well as how to appreciate and respect one another. Just make sure that over time all of the students are recognized for their efforts (and no student is recognized too often), as you do not want anyone to feel left out.

# LETTER TO THE EDITOR

Directions: Scan the newspaper and select an article you like. Based on the article, answer the questions below. Then write a friendly thank-you letter to the editor. Make sure to include your name and age at the end of your letter.

1. What is the title of the article you selected? _"Superintendent Doubles Recess"_

2. What is the author's name? _Bill Ding_

3. What is the page number of the article? _A15_

4. What is the date of the newspaper? _April 9, 2008_

5. Write your letter below.

_April 9, 2008_
[date]

Dear _Sharon Noledj_, Editor of _the Springfield Tribune:_
[editor's name]                           [newspaper]

Thank you for your article _"Superintendent Doubles Recess"_
[title of article]

by _Bill Ding_
[author's name]

on page _A15_ of the _April 9, 2008_, issue.

_I liked the article because I know the superintendent, Mr. Jones, and he helps students all the time._
[reason #1 why you enjoyed the article]

_Your article did a nice job of showing people how kind Mr. Jones is. He believes that children learn best when they play, and I agree._
[reason #2 why you enjoyed the article]

Keep up the great work!

Sincerely,

_Kesha Johnson_, age _8_
[your name]                [your age]

# LETTER TO THE EDITOR

Directions: Scan the newspaper and select an article you like. Based on the article, answer the questions below. Then write a friendly thank-you letter to the editor. Make sure to include your name and age at the end of your letter.

1. What is the title of the article you selected?_____

2. What is the author's name? _____

3. What is the page number of the article? _____

4. What is the date of the newspaper? _____

5. Write your letter below.

_____
      [date]

Dear _____, Editor of_____:
      [editor's name]              [newspaper]

Thank you for your article _____
                      [title of article]

by _____
[author's name]

on page _____ of the _____ , issue.
    [page number]        [date of newspaper]

_____
         [reason #1 why you enjoyed the article]

_____
         [reason #2 why you enjoyed the article]

Keep up the great work!

Sincerely,

_____, age _____
  [your name]            [your age]

# How Do I Look?

Good writers help readers smell, see, hear, taste, and feel what they are describing. This activity asks students to look for pictures in the newspaper and brainstorm in small groups all of the different ways they can describe the pictures. It's a great way to get your students to describe pictures with all five senses in mind. It's also a powerful way to engage your musical/rhythmic learners.

## WHAT YOU NEED

### FOR EACH STUDENT

- **scissors**
- **glue stick**
- **pencil**

### FOR EACH GROUP

- **newspaper**
- **construction paper**

### FOR THE TEACHER

- **music CDs or tapes**
- **CD or tape player**

## OBJECTIVE

Students will write brief expository descriptions of real objects, people, places, or events, using sensory details.

## PROCEDURE

1. Play different pieces of music and ask students to describe how the music affects their five senses (e.g., how the music makes them feel, what images they see).
2. Show students various pictures from the newspaper or from anywhere in the classroom. Ask students to come up with words that describe the pictures. (They do not have to be only adjectives.)
3. Ask them to work in groups of four or five.
4. Give each group one newspaper and several sheets of construction paper.
5. Make sure everyone has scissors, a glue stick, and a pencil.
6. Tell each group to scan the newspaper and cut out as many different pictures of objects, people, places, or events as they can find.
7. Explain that students should glue each cutout picture on a separate sheet of construction paper.
8. Ask each group to think of as many words as they can to describe each picture. Then have the students write the appropriate descriptive words on the back of the paper to which the picture is glued.
9. As a class, determine which group(s)

   a. found the greatest number of different photos;

   b. listed the most adjectives for a photo;

   c. used adjectives involving all five senses for a photo.

# Comical News

**M**ost students love comic strips. Encourage your students to read the comics daily and pay attention to what happens in different comics. Then have them summarize what took place in one comic strip. This is a great activity to train students how to sequence events and tell stories in three parts. It works well for developing students' oral skills, too. Try encouraging small groups to create their own "eyewitness news" broadcasts using the events in comic strips as news stories. You can also allow students to perform puppet news broadcasts, as some students are more likely to participate if they do not have to face their classmates. (They rarely show reluctance to narrate as puppets.)

## WHAT YOU NEED

### FOR EACH STUDENT

- **reproducible**
- **newspaper**
- **scissors**
- **glue stick**
- **pencil**

## OBJECTIVE

Students will write narratives that provide a context within which the action takes place, include well-chosen details to develop the plot, and provide insight into why the selected incident is memorable.

## PROCEDURE

1. Before class, make copies of the reproducible.
2. In class, hand out the newspapers and tell students to look at comic strips.
3. Give each student a copy of the reproducible.
4. Make sure everyone has scissors, a glue stick, and a pencil.
5. Explain that each student should select one comic strip from the newspaper, making sure the comic tells a story with a beginning, middle, and end.
6. Tell each student to follow the directions on the front of her reproducible and then glue the comic strip on the back.
7. Ask each student to find a partner. Have the partners share their stories with each other.
8. Ask student volunteers to share their stories with the class.

## Use Newspapers as Rewards

**T**he easiest way to spark the interest of young students in any activity is to offer the activity as a reward. When you place value on an item, your students will place value on it, too. Rather than using pizza and prizes to convince students to complete activities, tell them that they will get extra newspaper reading time, extra newspaper read-alouds by the teacher, or extra newspapers to take home. You can even encourage students to clip coupons and cash in those coupons for items from your "make and take" newspaper centers. I used to reward my students with many of the games we created for our centers.

# COMICAL NEWS

Directions: Answer the following questions about your comic strip, then write about what happened.

1. Why did you select this comic strip? _____

_____

2. What happens in the comic strip? _____

_____

3. Write a news story about what happens in your comic strip. Remember, a good news story contains a lead that answers the questions who, what, when, where, why, and how. Good supporting sentences describe why and how something happened.

_____

_____

_____

_____

_____

_____

_____

_____

_____

_____

_____

_____

# CHAPTER 9

# Writing Conventions

The question I hear from teachers more often than any other is, "How can I improve my students' spelling?" My standard response is this: give your students more time to read. For the purposes of this book, I encourage you to give your students more time to read newspapers. The more they see proper spelling, the more it will stick in their minds.

I have heard that among all professionals, the worst spellers are. . . drum roll . . . teachers. I can believe it. After all, teachers are constantly exposed to students' misspelled words. Humans naturally tend to adapt to their environments. Put a person around a bunch of smokers, and her likelihood of picking up smoking will greatly increase. I say, create a classroom filled with newspapers, discussions about newspapers, time spent reading newspapers, and opportunities to write for and about newspapers, and you will produce students who love reading and writing. Newspapers include a variety of writing formats. They model good grammar. And they have a significant advantage over most other print resources available to students: they are updated daily (or at least weekly). Newspapers capture students' interest with timely articles, and when students read newspapers—particularly the larger metropolitan ones—they are typically rewarded with examples of proper sentence structure, punctuation, spelling, capitalization, and grammar.

As an important part of most states' English/language-arts standards for grades 1–3, students are expected to write and speak with a command of grade-appropriate standard American English (academic language) conventions. The following mini-lessons are designed to help students to develop grade-appropriate spelling, punctuation, and syntax and an understanding of other writing conventions.

## Start a Class Dictionary

Dictionaries work best when students use them to check on words with which they already have some familiarity. Whenever students come across a challenging or new word in the newspaper, encourage them to highlight the word and cut out the sentence in which it appears. Ask students to glue each example on an index card that can then be added to a class dictionary. Whenever students find that same word in a different sentence, encourage them to write or glue the new example on the same card. I used to challenge my class to find at least five words a day to add to their class dictionary. Students felt more comfortable with the new vocabulary words because they saw the words used in different contexts, discussed the words' meanings with classmates, and related the words to their own personal experiences.

# Contraction Concentration

I am constantly trying to create lessons that demonstrate how you can turn any activity into a game. This one shows students how they can easily create their own memory-center games to practice contractions. Students can add their games to a classroom center or take them home to play with friends and family.

## WHAT YOU NEED

### FOR EACH STUDENT

- **newspaper**
- **index cards**
- **scissors**
- **glue stick**
- **pencil**

### FOR EACH PAIR

- **business envelope**

## OBJECTIVE

Students will identify and correctly use contractions.

## PROCEDURE

1. Review contractions with students.
2. Explain that newspapers tend to avoid using contractions in favor of spelling out words in their entirety. Point out, however, that contractions appear throughout the newspaper in quotations and advertisements.
3. Give each student a newspaper and a small stack of index cards.
4. Make sure everyone has scissors, a glue stick, and a pencil.
5. Ask students to scan their newspapers for contractions.
6. Explain that each student should cut out each contraction he finds and glue it on one of his index cards.
7. Tell each student to write the words that form each contraction on a separate card. For example, if he glues the word "can't" on one card, he should write "can" and "not" on another card.
8. Ask each student to find a partner.
9. Instruct the partners to review each other's contractions and words that form the contractions to ensure that they have completed the activity correctly. As a class, review examples from volunteers.
10. Ask students to pair off, then take all of their cards and put them facedown.
11. The game works like Concentration. To play, students take turns pulling two cards at a time. When a student chooses two cards that go together (e.g., one card with "can't" and one with "can" plus "not"), he gets to keep both cards.
12. Whoever has the most cards at the end of the game wins.
13. Hand out the business envelopes and ask students to place their cards in the envelopes so they can play the game again during center time.

## EXTRA! EXTRA!

You can create a Concentration memory game to reinforce just about any concept. I especially like creating centers that use this format to reinforce students' understanding of contractions, antonyms, and synonyms.

# You Complete Me

Students love to feel smarter than adults. Your students will get a kick out of finding incomplete sentences in the newspaper and "editing" them to turn them into complete sentences.

## WHAT YOU NEED

### FOR EACH STUDENT

- **reproducible**
- **yellow crayon**
- **pencil**
- **newspaper**

## OBJECTIVE

Students will distinguish between complete and incomplete sentences.

## PROCEDURE

1. Before class, make copies of the reproducible.
2. In class, review with students the differences between complete and incomplete sentences.
3. Point out to students that newspapers are filled with incomplete sentences (e.g., headlines, advertisements, classified ads).
4. Make sure everyone has a yellow crayon and a pencil.
5. Hand out the newspapers. Explain that each student should scan his copy for incomplete sentences and use the crayon to highlight as many as he can find.
6. Give each student a copy of the reproducible.
7. Explain that each student should copy in the appropriate places on the reproducible three of the incomplete sentences he highlighted in the newspaper. Add that he should write down the number of the page where he found each incomplete sentence.
8. Have each student rewrite each incomplete sentence as a complete sentence.
9. When everyone has finished, ask for volunteers to share their work with the class.

## EXTRA! EXTRA!

One way to prepare students for this activity—and to get students up and moving with a purpose—is to have board races in which you call students to the chalkboard to compete in teams. Reveal an incomplete sentence from the newspaper and have student teams compete as they change it into a complete sentence. You can also give students complete sentences and ask them to change them into headlines. You can judge the teams based on which one comes up with a complete sentence first, which one comes up with the best sentence, or some other criterion. Just make sure you tell your students what the goal is, or you may have a riot on your hands.

# You Complete Me

## INCOMPLETE SENTENCE #1                    Page _____

_____

Complete Sentence

_____

_____

## INCOMPLETE SENTENCE #2                    Page _____

_____

Complete Sentence

_____

_____

## INCOMPLETE SENTENCE #3                    Page _____

_____

Complete Sentence

_____

_____

# Punk-Shoo-A-Shun

**W**hen children are first learning to write, many become obsessed with exclamation points. As a result, their sentences lack variety and demand to be read with undue emphasis: I like school! I like my friends! I like my teacher! The end! Students enjoy it when you read sentences and exaggerate the tone of your voice to match different forms of punctuation.

## WHAT YOU NEED

### FOR EACH STUDENT

- **reproducible**
- **newspaper**
- **scissors**
- **glue stick**

## OBJECTIVE

Students will use periods, exclamation points, and question marks properly at the end of sentences.

## PROCEDURE

1. Before class, make copies of the reproducible.
2. In class, point out to students a specific sentence in the newspaper (e.g., "Police say the suspect stole more than $500").
3. Ask students to recite the sentence together.
4. Ask them what would happen if you were to change the end punctuation.
5. Give students a chance to recite the same sentence with different forms of end punctuation. Encourage them to change their tone of voice to reflect the different punctuation marks.
6. Hand out all of the materials.
7. Explain that students should scan the newspaper for sentences with different types of punctuation.
8. Ask each student to cut out at least one example of a sentence that uses a period, one that uses an exclamation point, and one that uses a question mark.
9. Instruct students to glue their samples in the appropriate boxes on the reproducible.
10. Ask students to look in their newspapers for examples of sentences using other punctuation marks and to glue those in the box at the bottom of the reproducible.
11. Have students pair off and practice reading their sentences to their partners.
12. Instruct students to try changing the punctuation at the end of each sentence to see if that changes the way they read the sentence.
13. As a class, practice changing punctuation.

## EXTRA! EXTRA!

Ask students to scan the newspaper and highlight different types of sentences with different-colored crayons. In particular, tell students that newspapers use exclamation points infrequently. Ask students to look at their highlighting to see if they can tell what section of the newspaper uses the most exclamation points. (It's usually the sports section.)

# PUNK-SHOO-A-SHUN

Period (.)

Question Mark (?)

Exclamation Point (!)

Other Punctuation Marks

# Nouns All Around

I t's not just the words in newspapers that support learning. This activity uses newspaper pictures to reinforce students' recognition of different types of nouns. When completed, it will provide the materials for a very effective center activity, too.

## WHAT YOU NEED

### FOR EACH STUDENT

- **pencil**
- **scissors**
- **glue stick**
- **crayons**
- **paper**
- **newspaper**

### FOR THE TEACHER

- **marker**
- **butcher paper**
- **pictures of people, places, and things**

## OBJECTIVE

Students will identify nouns in writing and speaking.

## PROCEDURE

1. Before class, write "Person" at the top of one sheet of butcher paper, "Place" at the top of a second sheet, and "Thing" at the top of a third. Post all three sheets in the classroom.

2. Review the concept of nouns as a class. Show students pictures of people, places, and things and ask students to identify them.

3. Glue the pictures on the appropriate sheets of butcher paper. Label each picture with the name (noun) the students suggested (e.g., police officer, dancer).

4. Make sure everyone has a pencil, scissors, a glue stick, and crayons.

5. Give each student three sheets of paper. Ask him to label one "Person," one "Place," and one "Thing."

6. Hand out the newspapers and ask students to scan them for pictures that represent different types of nouns.

7. Explain that each student is to cut out one example of each type of noun (person, place, thing) and glue each example on the appropriate sheet of paper.

8. Ask students to write the correct name (noun) under each picture.

9. Explain that each student should draw on each sheet of paper pictures of at least four other nouns that are appropriate for that category. Have them write the correct name under each drawing.

10. Tell students to glue their noun groupings on the appropriate sheets of butcher paper.

11. As a class, brainstorm a list of nouns. As students come up with suggestions, write each on the appropriate sheet of butcher paper.

12. Review the list as a class. If you like, leave the butcher paper up on the wall for the week and review the nouns every day. Then roll the sheets up for use in a center (see box).

## EXTRA! EXTRA!

Another way to reinforce students' understanding of parts of speech is to ask each student to copy a story from the newspaper and replace specific items (e.g., name of city, type of fruit) with blanks. Then have students work in pairs to create their own "Mad Lib" exercises.

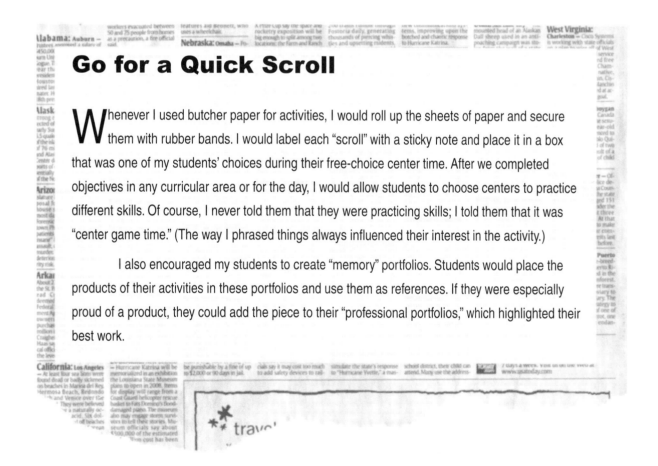

## Go for a Quick Scroll

Whenever I used butcher paper for activities, I would roll up the sheets of paper and secure them with rubber bands. I would label each "scroll" with a sticky note and place it in a box that was one of my students' choices during their free-choice center time. After we completed objectives in any curricular area or for the day, I would allow students to choose centers to practice different skills. Of course, I never told them that they were practicing skills; I told them that it was "center game time." (The way I phrased things always influenced their interest in the activity.)

I also encouraged my students to create "memory" portfolios. Students would place the products of their activities in these portfolios and use them as references. If they were especially proud of a product, they could add the piece to their "professional portfolios," which highlighted their best work.

# Sentence Skylines

**I**t is important to provide activities that allow students with different talents to succeed. Your logical/mathematical and visual/spatial learners will appreciate this exercise because it allows them to graphically illustrate their comprehension of different sentence types. All of your students will enjoy the change of pace.

## WHAT YOU NEED

### FOR EACH STUDENT

- **reproducible**
- **newspaper**
- **scissors**
- **glue stick**
- **crayons**

## OBJECTIVE

Students will recognize complete and correct declarative, interrogative, and exclamatory sentences in writing and speaking.

## PROCEDURE

1. Before class, make copies of the reproducible.
2. In class, review declarative, interrogative, and exclamatory sentences with students.
3. Review how changing the punctuation at the end of a sentence can completely change the meaning.
4. Tell students that newspapers contain examples of different types of sentences: sentences that state facts (declarative), sentences that ask questions (interrogative), and even sentences that express excitement (exclamatory). Point out that newspapers typically do not include many exclamatory sentences except in ads.
5. Ask students to pair off.

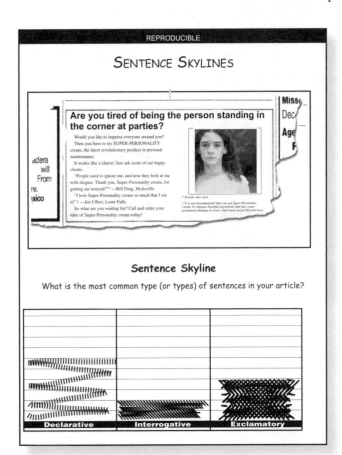

6. Give each student (not each pair) a newspaper and a copy of the reproducible.
7. Make sure everyone has scissors, a glue stick, and crayons.
8. Ask each student to scan the newspaper; cut out an advertisement, editorial, or article; and glue it on her reproducible.
9. Tell students to highlight sentences in their articles with crayons, shading each declarative sentence in orange, each interrogative sentence in yellow, and each exclamatory sentence in light green.
10. Direct students to shade in a box for each sentence in the appropriate column of their Sentence Skyline graphs. Tell them to use the same colors in the graph as they did for the highlighting.
11. Ask each student to share her Sentence Skyline with a partner and discuss which type or types of sentences dominate her newspaper item.
12. Ask volunteers to provide examples of the types of sentences they found with the class.

# SENTENCE SKYLINES

Glue the newspaper item here.

## Sentence Skyline

What is the most common type (or types) of sentences in your article?

| Declarative | Interrogative | Exclamatory |
| --- | --- | --- |
| | | |
| | | |
| | | |
| | | |
| | | |
| | | |
| | | |
| | | |
| | | |
| | | |
| | | |
| | | |

# Constant Action

Students love card games. This one works much like the game Uno. Rather than dealing with colors and numbers, however, this version reinforces students' knowledge of verbs and their tenses. It's a great way for students to interact with one another as they practice verb tenses in a fun way, rather than by "drill and kill" methods.

## WHAT YOU NEED

### FOR EACH STUDENT

- **scissors**
- **glue stick**
- **red crayon**
- **pencil**
- **index cards**

### FOR EACH GROUP

- **newspaper**
- **manila envelope**

## OBJECTIVE

Students will identify and use past, present, and future verb tenses properly in writing and speaking.

## PROCEDURE

1. Talk about the card game Uno with students. (If you have the game, giving students a chance to play it is even better.) Explain how that game reviews colors and numbers. Tell students that they are going to create their own kind of Uno game, using verbs and tenses.

2. Review past, present, and future tenses of verbs with students.

3. Point out to students that newspapers feature a lot of strong verbs in headlines to attract readers.

4. Ask students to work in groups of four or five.

5. Hand out the newspapers and explain that each group should divide the sections of the newspaper among the members.

6. Make sure everyone has scissors, a glue stick, a red crayon, and a pencil.

7. Instruct students to scan the headlines in their newspapers and cut out as many verbs as they can find. Encourage them to look for examples of all tenses.

8. Hand out the index cards and tell students to glue each headline verb on a different index card. The goal is for each student (*not* each group) to create at least ten verb cards.

9. Direct students to use a red crayon to write the tense of each verb on the back of the card. For example, if the student cuts out "run," she would write "present" on the back of the index card.

10. Underneath that, tell students to write in pencil the past, present, and future tenses of the verb. Using the example in step 9, the student would write "ran, run, will run" under the word "present."

11. Explain that one student in each group should write the word "begin" on a card. Ask the student to write the tense of that verb in red crayon on the back of the card, along with the past, present, and future tenses ("began," "begin," "will begin") in pencil. Each group needs to make one of these cards, which will act as the beginning card for the game.

12. Have all of the students in each group put their cards together in one stack.

13. Ask each group to review their stack together to check for accuracy. If a group has a question about any verb or tense, they should ask you for assistance.

14. Have one person in each group shuffle the cards and then deal them, distributing the cards equally among the members of the group.

15. Instruct students to hold their cards so that others can't see them.

16. Explain the game to the class. The person with the handwritten "begin" card starts play by putting that card down with the one-word side up. Play continues clockwise around the group. The next person must lay down a card on top of the "begin" card that either (1) shows the same tense (in this case, present) or (2) shows another tense of the word (in this case, "began" or "will begin") that is on top of the stack. If the player does not have a card that follows either of those rules, he must skip his turn. Students always place their cards on the stack with the one-word side up. If a student wants to question a play, he should look at the back of the card to see if the word is in the same tense as the previous verb or is another tense of that verb. The winner is the first person to get rid of all of his cards.

17. Hand out the manila envelopes. Have each group place their cards in a manila envelope so that they can play the game again later.

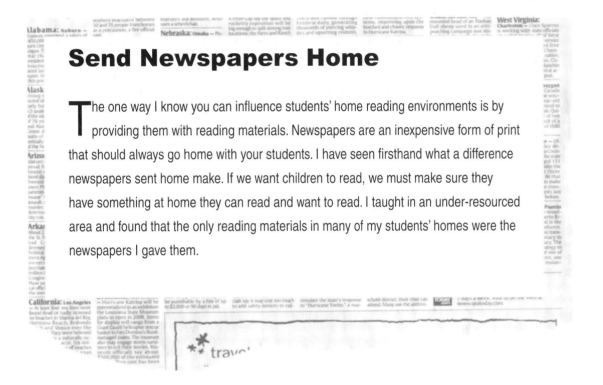

# Send Newspapers Home

The one way I know you can influence students' home reading environments is by providing them with reading materials. Newspapers are an inexpensive form of print that should always go home with your students. I have seen firsthand what a difference newspapers sent home make. If we want children to read, we must make sure they have something at home they can read and want to read. I taught in an under-resourced area and found that the only reading materials in many of my students' homes were the newspapers I gave them.

# Alpha Order

This activity is a fun way to demonstrate to students that writing has to be organized. Show students how newspapers organize information into categories (e.g., news, sports, editorials) and alphabetically (in the index).

## WHAT YOU NEED

### FOR EACH STUDENT

- **reproducible**
- **newspaper**
- **scissors**
- **pencil**
- **manila envelope**

## OBJECTIVE

Students will determine how to find categories, place words into different categories, and arrange words in alphabetical order.

## PROCEDURE

1. Before class, make copies of the reproducible.

2. In class, discuss with students the importance of organization. For example, point out that newspapers keep sports stories in the sports section rather than with the weather one day and the classified ads another day.

3. Remind students that they can use newspapers to practice classifying things and placing them in alphabetical order.

4. Hand out all of the materials.

5. Tell students that they need to think of a way of classifying newspaper information. Each student may choose any category she'd like (e.g., sports, foods in grocery store ads, movie titles, headlines, jobs, famous names) and then come up with words in the newspaper that fit that category. Ask students to focus on words in headlines, but add that if they cannot find words in headlines, they may use words from within stories as well. Encourage students to get creative.

6. Instruct each student to write the name of his category at the top of the empty box on the reproducible.

7. Ask students to cut their words out of the newspaper and arrange them in alphabetical order. Then have them copy their words onto the reproducible, writing them in alphabetical order in the large box.

8. Ask students to place the cutout words in their manila envelopes. Then have them cut out the boxes they've completed and paste them on the back of their envelopes.

9. Ask each student to find a partner and exchange envelopes with the partner.

10. Tell each partner to empty the words out of the envelope and place the envelope facedown so that he cannot see the name of the category or how the words are arranged. Then have him work with the cutout words, arranging them in alphabetical order.

11. When the student is done, have him tell his partner what category he thinks the words belong to.

12. Allow the partner to turn the envelope over to see if he guessed the correct category and placed the cutouts correctly in alphabetical order. Students get credit if they come close to guessing a category correctly. For instance, if the correct category is "foods" and the partner guesses "vegetables," he will get credit if all of the words are vegetables.

13. Share as a class.

# ALPHA ORDER

**Example:**

**Classification:** _____
                         Sports

Baseball
Basketball
Football
Golf
Hockey
Horse racing
NASCAR racing
Soccer

**Classification:** _____

# Big Time

**B**igger is better! Students typically love to work with capital letters, and this is a great way to get them to pay attention to capitalization. You can easily build on this activity and integrate capitalization into your morning meeting by intentionally not capitalizing students' names, days of the week, and other proper nouns and letting students correct your "mistakes."

## WHAT YOU NEED

### FOR EACH STUDENT

- **reproducible**
- **newspaper**
- **yellow crayon**
- **pencil**

### FOR THE TEACHER

- **markers**
- **butcher paper**

## OBJECTIVE

Students will correctly capitalize all proper nouns (e.g., months, days of the week, people's names and titles, place names) and words at the beginning of sentences.

## PROCEDURE

1. Before class, make copies of the reproducible.
2. From the newspaper, select a specific article that contains each type of capitalization listed on the reproducible (words that begin sentences; people's names, titles, or initials; place names; names of months, days of the week, holidays, and special events).
3. Use markers to create one butcher paper chart for each of these four categories. Post the charts at the front of the room.
4. As a class, review different uses of capitalization.
5. Give each student a newspaper and a copy of the reproducible.
6. Make sure everyone has a yellow crayon and a pencil.
7. Direct students to the specific newspaper article you have chosen.
8. Explain that each student should highlight with the crayon each capitalized word she encounters in the article.
9. Ask students to pair off.
10. Point out the four charts at the front of the room. Ask each student to whisper to her partner four capitalized words in the article—one for each category.
11. Ask student volunteers to share examples of the capitalized words they whispered to their partners. Let each volunteer write one word on the appropriate sheet of butcher paper with a marker.
12. Tell students to copy the words they highlighted in the article in the proper boxes on the reproducible.
13. Review as a class.
14. On the butcher paper charts at the front of the room, write the rest of the words the students found. Keep these charts posted throughout the year for students to use as visual reminders.

## EXTRA! EXTRA!

Encourage students to create their own stories that use different types of capitalized words. Challenge students to write sentences that include an example of each type of capitalized word they found in the newspaper.

---

REPRODUCIBLE

### BIG TIME

1. Capitalized Words That Begin Sentences

The
Some
In

2. Capitalized Names, Titles, or Initials of People

T.R.
Mayor
Coach
Arnold Schwarzenegger

3. Capitalized Place Names

Springfield
Rocky Mountains
City Hall

4. Capitalized Names of Months, Days of the Week, Holidays, and Special Events

March
Tuesday
Thanksgiving
Super Bowl

# BIG TIME

1. Capitalized Words That Begin Sentences

2. Capitalized Names, Titles, or Initials of People

3. Capitalized Place Names

4. Capitalized Names of Months, Days of the Week, Holidays, and Special Events

# Listening & Speaking

**CHAPTER 10**

Have you ever been around a person who constantly corrects the way you speak? My guess is that you try to avoid that person. Why, then, do so many teachers feel compelled to correct their students' language?

I love newspapers. I love my grandfather, too. My grandfather is not perfect, and newspapers are not perfect either. Students need to see that even role models have flaws, and newspapers are no different. You can look at any newspaper on any day, and you'll find mistakes in grammar, mislabeled photographs, and other "glaring" errors. Students need to see that even a newspaper, a document that has likely been edited by at least four people, contains occasional blunders. Students need to know that it is all right to make mistakes. In fact, making mistakes is essential to learning. People who avoid risks never experience the satisfaction of improvement through effort. Encourage your students to ask lots of questions and to comment on the newspaper items they read. Silent voices are never heard.

I have taught a lot of students who immigrated to America (ESL students), and I have found that facilitating silly games with newspapers often encourages timid ESL students to practice speaking. Many of these students are familiar with some news stories because they have read about them in their native-language newspapers or have seen reports about them on native-language television stations. Often they are drawn to English-language newspaper reports on the same stories because they already have some understanding of the topics. We know that prior knowledge builds confidence, and confidence leads to participation. When I work on speaking and listening standards with first, second, and third graders, my goal is not to see students practice perfect English. I want to see students practice, period.

Newspapers, better than any other printed resource I know, engage students in speaking and listening.

Many states' English/language-arts standards for grades 1–3 require students to be able to listen critically and respond appropriately to oral communication. Additionally, students typically must demonstrate a command of standard American English (academic language) and speak in a manner that guides listeners to understand important ideas. They're expected to do this by using proper phrasing, organization, pitch, and modulation. The following mini-lessons are meant to encourage students to listen carefully to newspaper stories and articulate their reactions to what they read in newspapers.

# Planning Your Vacation

This is a good way to get your students excited about visiting different areas of the United States. Note that it does require students to use travel information. Although not all newspapers have travel sections, most contain plenty of articles about faraway places or advertisements for travel services. Become familiar with your local newspaper's format so that you can properly direct your students to the right section(s) of the newspaper. That way, students will be better equipped to determine where to search their newspapers for particular pieces of information and supporting details.

Note that if your local newspaper is not published daily or does not include a weather map, you can always use the map from *USA Today*.

## WHAT YOU NEED

### FOR EACH STUDENT

- **reproducible**
- **newspaper**
- **scissors**
- **glue stick**
- **crayons**
- **pencil**

## OBJECTIVE

Students will report on a topic with facts and details, drawing from several sources of information.

## PROCEDURE

1. Before class, make copies of the reproducible.
2. In class, tell students that each of them is going to plan a trip anywhere in the United States.
3. Hand out the newspapers and instruct students to use their newspapers to help them plan their trips. Tell them that they may cut photos and advertisements out of the newspaper to help in their planning.
4. Give each student a copy of the reproducible.
5. Make sure everyone has scissors, a glue stick, crayons, and a pencil.
6. Ask each student to cut out the national weather map from the newspaper and glue it in the box on the reproducible, then use a crayon to draw a star marking the location she'd like to visit.
7. Instruct students to answer the questions on the reproducible. Explain that they may choose to write the answers or to cut out pictures and advertisements from the newspaper and glue those in place instead. For example, a student might use a picture of an airplane to indicate his answer to the question about how he will get to his destination.
8. Ask students to pair off and discuss their travel plans with their partners.
9. Ask student volunteers to share their travel plans with the class.

## EXTRA! EXTRA!

Encourage your students to write (or e-mail) different tourist bureaus and chambers of commerce to ask for brochures, maps, and information about attractions. I have found that AAA (American Automobile Association) is willing to supply teachers with maps, travel books, posters of various locales, etc. The more you can pump your students up about their travel plans, the more likely they will be to present interesting oral talks about their vacation ideas.

# Develop a Class Map

Geography is often neglected in our schools, so I love integrating geography into my English/language-arts lessons. Hang a U.S. map and a world map on one of your bulletin boards. Challenge students to find stories in the newspaper that take place in different locations. Allow them to mark the location of each place they read about with a pushpin or sticker. You can also show students newspapers from other parts of the country (pull those papers off the Internet, if you like) and discuss what stories are important to people in different regions. For instance, traffic news may be important in cities, but crop reports may be more important in rural areas.

# PLANNING YOUR VACATION

Glue the weather map here.

1. Where are you going?_____

_____

2. How are you going to get there? _____

_____

3. What do you want to see and do there? _____

_____

_____

4. How much will the trip cost? _____

5. What kind of clothes do you need to pack? _____

_____

_____

# My Take on This

Providing students with opportunities to share their experiences with one another is a great way to develop language skills. If you have students who speak languages other than English in your classroom (ESL students), allow them to relate experiences to one another in their primary language, if they wish. I observed that the more opportunities I gave my ESL students to communicate in their primary language, the quicker and smoother their transition to English became. But this activity is not just for ESL students; it is meant to allow all of your students to share their experiences with one another.

## WHAT YOU NEED

### FOR EACH STUDENT

- **newspaper**
- **scissors**
- **glue stick**
- **paper**

## OBJECTIVE

Students will connect and relate their experiences, insights, and ideas to those of a speaker.

## PROCEDURE

1. Hand out the newspapers.
2. Make sure everyone has scissors, a glue stick, and paper.
3. Ask students to scan their newspapers for interesting articles and photos.
4. Tell each student to cut out three articles or photos—one that makes her sad, one that makes her laugh, and one that makes her think.
5. Tell each student to glue her selections on a sheet of paper.
6. Ask students to pair off and share with their partners the articles or photos they chose.
7. Add that while one student is explaining why she chose an article or photo, the partner who's listening may interrupt only to ask questions. When the student has finished explaining, the partner may say how the article affected her.
8. Share as a class.

## EXTRA! EXTRA!

Now that your students have had some practice finding materials that interest them in the newspaper, recommend that they routinely cut out articles and photos they like and glue them in their writer's journals. Point out that if they do that, they'll always have ideas for interesting things to write about.

Encourage students to keep track of their experiences in other ways, too. For example, they may draw pictures about their experiences, chart similar experiences, or write songs about experiences. All of these ways of recording will give them good subjects for future writing projects.

# Treasure Hunt

**S**tudents love searching for information based on directions. This activity allows each student to give oral clues that a classmate can follow to solve the "mystery": which part of the newspaper the student is describing.

## WHAT YOU NEED

### FOR EACH STUDENT

- **newspaper**
- **paper**
- **pencil**

## OBJECTIVE

Students will determine the purposes of listening (e.g., to obtain information, to solve problems, for enjoyment).

## PROCEDURE

1. Review with students how newspapers serve different purposes (e.g., reporting news, providing information about upcoming events, expressing opinions).
2. Ask each student to find a partner.
3. Read aloud different parts of the newspaper (e.g., a classified ad, a movie review, a crime story).
4. After you read each example, ask students to tell their partners if the passage was meant to be read for enjoyment, to convey information, or to solve a problem.
5. Share students' answers as a class, and encourage students to explain their answers.
6. Hand out all of the materials.
7. Tell students that they are going to create their own treasure hunts. The purpose of the activity is to create instructions that another person can follow to find specific information in the newspaper. Instructions can be written or oral, or they can be acted out or drawn.
8. Tell each student to choose a specific item in the newspaper (e.g., the crossword puzzle, an ad for margarine, a photo of a football player scoring a touchdown).
9. Have each student create instructions for how to get to the item he has selected, then ask a question about a specific piece of information in the item.
10. Ask each student to choose a partner to follow his instructions and see if the partner can find the item and answer the question.
11. Ask for volunteers to share their instructions with the class, then review those instructions together.

## Treasure Hunt

1. Turn to the sports section.
2. Go to the back, where it says "NBA box scores."
3. Look for the box score under "L.A. Lakers."
4. Find the line that says "Bryant."
5. Can you find out how many points Kobe Bryant scored last night?

# Facts & Go Figure

This game encourages students to pay attention to how newspapers include both facts and opinions in articles. Students enjoy playing the game, and it gets them to pay attention to where information comes from. This can lead to other activities that deal with how students evaluate information, including how they view themselves. (For example, if a person says you are ugly, do you believe it to be a fact or consider it that person's opinion?)

## WHAT YOU NEED

### FOR EACH STUDENT

- **reproducible**
- **newspaper**
- **pencil**

## OBJECTIVE

Students will distinguish between opinions and verifiable facts.

## PROCEDURE

1. Before class, look over the reproducible. If necessary, modify it to make it appropriate for the newspaper you're using. Make a copy for each student.

2. In class, tell students that newspapers contain facts and opinions. Discuss ways to determine whether a story is an opinion piece or a factual article.

3. Point out that facts can be proved, are true for all people and places, and can be observed. Explain that opinions, by contrast, refer to a particular person's (or group's) feelings, thoughts, judgments, and beliefs. Read aloud several selections from the newspaper and ask students whether each is fact or opinion.

4. Explain to students that just because an important person (e.g., a politician, a coach) is quoted as saying something, it does not necessarily mean that what the person says is true. Point out that newspapers often poll readers about their opinions on certain matters and then report their findings as facts.

5. Make a series of statements to students and have students discuss whether each is fact or opinion (e.g., broccoli is green, broccoli is nasty, broccoli contains many nutritious vitamins).

6. Hand out all of the materials.

7. Instruct students to scan the newspaper for the items listed on the reproducible. Explain that, after looking at each type of item, students should decide whether it is based on fact or opinion. They should then put an *X* in the appropriate box.

8. When all of the students have completed the reproducible, ask them to pair off and share their charts with their partners.

9. Ask one student in each pair to read aloud one sentence from each article. Her partner must guess whether it is a statement of fact or opinion.

10. Have the partners reverse roles and repeat.

11. Discuss as a class. Ask students if they found any articles that contained both facts and opinions.

## EXTRA! EXTRA!

I used to play a game with my students called Two Truths, One Lie. Students pair off, and one student in each pair makes three statements. Two of the statements must be true, and one must be a lie. The object of the game is for the partner to determine which statement is a lie. Two Truths, One Lie is a fun icebreaker to use before this activity to encourage students to share their experiences with one another.

# Facts & Go Figure

| | Fact | Opinion |
|---|---|---|
| 1. Letter to the editor | | |
| 2. Movie review | | |
| 3. Front-page news story | | |
| 4. Sports box score | | |
| 5. Date | | |
| 6. Horoscope | | |
| 7. Wedding announcement | | |
| 8. Obituary | | |
| 9. Weather forecast | | |
| 10. Sunrise | | |
| 11. Editorial | | |
| 12. Movie times | | |
| 13. Cost of the newspaper | | |
| 14. Advice column | | |
| 15. Dateline | | |
| 16. Byline | | |
| 17. Index | | |
| 18. Sports column | | |
| 19. Restaurant review | | |

# Picture Password

This works a lot like the game Taboo, only for younger children. Students enjoy finding pictures in the newspaper and trying to describe them in as few words as possible in order to get people to guess what the picture is. This is a great way to get students to use all of their senses when describing items.

## WHAT YOU NEED

### FOR EACH STUDENT

- **reproducible**
- **newspaper**
- **scissors**
- **glue stick**
- **pencil**

## OBJECTIVE

Students will use concrete sensory details to describe people, places, things, or experiences.

## PROCEDURE

1. Before class, make copies of the reproducible.

2. Point out to students that many people enjoy newspaper feature stories for how they describe people, places, things, and experiences. A good feature story tends to appeal to a broad range of senses and emotions (e.g., a story about chocolate chip cookies can leave your mouth watering; a story about a baby being kidnapped can make you feel sad).

3. Add that students can make their own writing and speaking more interesting by using rich descriptions. For instance, you can say that something smells "gross" or describe it as reeking of gym socks and boiled liver.

4. Hand out all of the materials.

5. Ask each student to scan the newspaper and cut out a photo, then glue the picture on her reproducible.

6. Explain that each student is to write down as many sensory and emotional words as she can think of to describe her photo. She should write each word in the appropriate column on the reproducible.

7. Ask students to find partners.

8. Explain that each student, without showing her picture to her partner, must provide one word at a time to describe the picture to her partner.

9. Add that the partner may look at photos throughout his copy of the same newspaper. He must then guess, based on the clues given, what the picture is.

10. Ask the partners to swap roles and repeat the process.

11. Tell students that the winner of the game is the one who can get her partner to guess the correct picture with the fewest clues.

12. Ask volunteers to share their clues with the class and see how the class does at guessing each picture.

REPRODUCIBLE

PICTURE PASSWORD

| Sensory Words | | | | | Emotional Words |
|---|---|---|---|---|---|
| Smell | Taste | Sight | Hearing | Touch | |
|  |  |  |  |  |  |
| sweaty |  | helmet | cheers | hard | excited |
| grass |  | football |  |  | celebrates |
|  |  |  |  |  |  |
|  |  |  |  |  |  |
|  |  |  |  |  |  |
|  |  |  |  |  |  |

# PICTURE PASSWORD

Glue the photo here.

| Sensory Words | | | | | Emotional Words |
|---|---|---|---|---|---|
| Smell | Taste | Sight | Hearing | Touch | |
| | | | | | |
| | | | | | |
| | | | | | |
| | | | | | |
| | | | | | |
| | | | | | |
| | | | | | |
| | | | | | |

# Act It Out

**F**irst, second, and third graders need to move around. Your students will love this activity because it enables them to act silly in front of one another. It is also a great way to determine what background knowledge your students have about specific subjects they are about to study.

## WHAT YOU NEED

### FOR EACH STUDENT

- **reproducible**
- **newspaper**
- **pencil**

## OBJECTIVE

Students will plan and present dramatic interpretations of experiences or stories.

## PROCEDURE

1. Before class, make copies of the reproducible.

2. In class, explain that stories in newspapers often provide inspiration for novelists and for television and movie writers.

3. Point out to students that any program that claims to be "based on a true story" probably was first reported in the newspaper. In particular, writers turn to crime stories, disaster stories, and inspirational stories from newspapers to get ideas for novels, movies, and TV shows.

4. Ask students to form groups of four or five.

5. Give each student a newspaper and a copy of the reproducible. Make sure everyone has a pencil.

6. Tell students that they will work on the activity in groups, but that each student is responsible for filling out her own reproducible.

7. Explain that each group should scan their newspapers and find a story that the group would like to act out. You may want to choose one article for all of your students the first few times so that students will have the opportunity to see how different groups interpret the article.

8. Tell students to copy their group's headline on the reproducible and answer the questions there.

9. Explain that each group is to work from what they've learned in the article to create a skit for the class telling their story. Remind students that every member of each group must participate.

10. Allow each group to share their article's headline, main characters, and setting with the class, then act out their skit. If some students are shy, have limited English-language skills, or just do not like speaking in front of a group, allow them to perform without speaking, if they wish. They can demonstrate their knowledge with their gestures.

11. Discuss with the class whether they would like to see alternative endings to any of the stories. Allow students to act out different endings.

## EXTRA! EXTRA!

This can be a great activity for solidifying students' understanding of new vocabulary words. Encourage students to incorporate new words into their skits.

# Act It Out

Newspaper story headline: _____

Where does your story take place? _____

When does your story take place? _____

What happens in the story?

_____

_____

Who are the characters in your story, and who will play their parts?

_____

_____

_____

_____

What emotions do you want the audience to feel?

_____

_____

_____

_____

Is there anything you would like to change about the story for your presentation?

_____

_____

_____

_____

Note: Make sure to tell the class about the characters and setting before you perform your skit.

# Daily Order

**Y**oung students appreciate predictable routines. This activity gets students thinking about the predictable patterns they encounter daily and weekly (e.g., in newspapers, at home, during class). It also can be integrated into health lessons that encourage daily habits such as bathing, grooming, brushing teeth, eating breakfast, and getting enough sleep. If your local newspaper does not contain sections that feature instructions, download examples from major newspapers on the Internet (see page 137).

## WHAT YOU NEED

### FOR EACH STUDENT

- **reproducible**
- **newspaper**
- **pencil**
- **crayons**

## OBJECTIVE

Students will recount experiences in a logical sequence by organizing ideas chronologically or around major points of information.

## PROCEDURE

1. Before class, make copies of the reproducible.
2. In class, explain to students that newspapers often feature articles that teach people how to do certain things (e.g., recipe instructions, home maintenance tips, advice for what to do during a hurricane).
3. Hand out the newspapers.
4. Together, look at different sections of the newspaper that provide instructions.
5. Tell each student to find a partner.
6. Make sure everyone has a pencil and crayons.
7. Ask the pairs to scan sections of the newspaper and pay attention to the order in which information appears within each section.
8. Show students examples of the newspaper from each day of the week and ask if the order within each section of the newspaper changes from day to day or if the section follows a predictable routine (e.g., box scores are always at the back of the sports section, help wanted ads are always at the beginning of the classified section, letters to the editor are always on the right-hand editorial page).
9. Ask students to discuss any part of their daily or weekly routines at home or at school.
10. Hand out the copies of the reproducible.
11. Instruct each student to choose one of his daily or weekly routines. Then have him write and/or draw five steps from the routine, in order, on the reproducible.
12. Tell students to share their routines with their partners.
13. Ask volunteers to share their routines with the class.

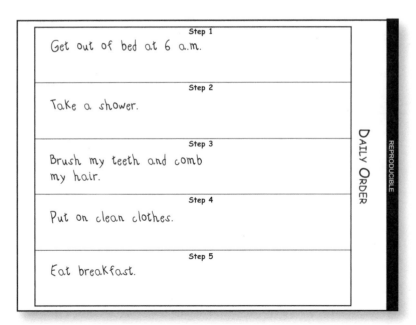

# Daily Order

| Step 1 | Step 2 | Step 3 | Step 4 | Step 5 |
|--------|--------|--------|--------|--------|
|        |        |        |        |        |

# An Edible Lesson

It is always fun to practice chronological order by allowing students to create recipes. My students and I used to enjoy following the directions to make a peanut butter and jelly sandwich. The students would work in pairs: one would give the directions, while the other would follow them to the letter. Inevitably, the student giving the directions would skip an important step (e.g., remove the peanut butter from the jar), producing funny consequences.

# Newspaper Diamantes

**P**oetry is one of my favorite means of getting students excited about school. Poems, like newspapers, are typically pretty succinct. They follow a variety of styles, and students typically enjoy reciting them. You can use variations of this activity to reinforce students' familiarity with other types of poetry, too. Try it with ballads, haiku, acrostics, and limericks.

## WHAT YOU NEED

### FOR EACH STUDENT

- **reproducible**
- **newspaper**
- **pencil**

### FOR THE TEACHER

- **marker**
- **butcher paper**

## OBJECTIVE

Students will recite poems and provide descriptions with careful attention to sensory details.

## PROCEDURE

1. Before class, make copies of the reproducible.
2. In class, explain that newspapers provide plenty of subjects for writing poems.
3. Remind students that the best poems appeal to people's senses and emotions. Read aloud a couple of newspaper stories and ask students to share how the stories made them feel.
4. Remind students of different types of poems they have read and written (e.g., haiku). Then focus on the specific structure of a diamante as outlined in the reproducible.
5. Hand out the newspapers.
6. Make sure everyone has a pencil.
7. Select a newspaper story as a class. On butcher paper, create a diamante for that story.
8. Give each student a copy of the reproducible.
9. Ask students to look for stories and photos in the newspaper that appeal to their emotions or senses.
10. Explain that each student should choose one of those stories or photos, then write on the reproducible a list of words that relate to the subject of the story or photo.
11. Ask each student to use the words he has written to create a diamante. Remind students that a diamante is shaped like a diamond and follows a specific seven-line structure, as outlined in the reproducible.

---

REPRODUCIBLE

### NEWSPAPER DIAMANTES

| |
|---|
| Line 1: One word—subject, noun |
| Line 2: Two words—adjectives describing line 1 |
| Line 3: Three words—participles (-ing form) related to line 1 |
| Line 4: Four words—nouns, two related to line 1, two related to line 7 |
| Line 5: Three words—participles related to line 7 |
| Line 6: Two words—adjectives describing line 7 |
| Line 7: One word—noun, opposite of subject in line 1 |

Newspaper story headline: _Hurricane Horatio Pounds the Coast_

Words that relate to your story:

| | | | | |
|---|---|---|---|---|
| hurricane | furious | storm | pounding | violent |
| rain | fast | scary | destroy | terrifying |
| disaster | unexpected | volunteers | beach | help |
| debris | peace | flood | damage | water |
| aid | charity | pray | calm | silence |
| unite | cooperate | quiet | still | |

**Diamante**

1.                     Hurricane
2.              fast        furious
3.          raining    damaging    terrifying
4.    storm    disaster    calm    silence
5.        praying    uniting    cooperating
6.            quiet    still
7                   Peace

12. Ask students to pair off and share their poems with their partners.

13. Allow student volunteers to share their diamantes with the class.

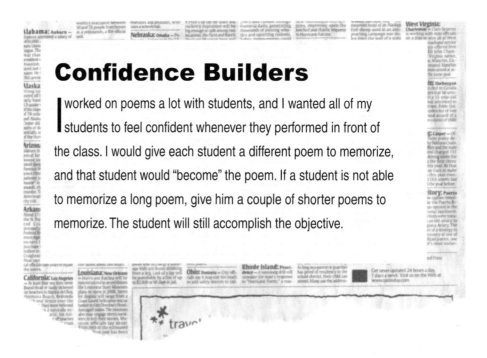

## Confidence Builders

I worked on poems a lot with students, and I wanted all of my students to feel confident whenever they performed in front of the class. I would give each student a different poem to memorize, and that student would "become" the poem. If a student is not able to memorize a long poem, give him a couple of shorter poems to memorize. The student will still accomplish the objective.

# Newspaper Diamantes

| |
|---|
| Line 1: One word—subject, noun |
| Line 2: Two words—adjectives describing line 1 |
| Line 3: Three words—participles (-ing form) related to line 1 |
| Line 4: Four words—nouns, two related to line 1, two related to line 7 |
| Line 5: Three words—participles related to line 7 |
| Line 6: Two words—adjectives describing line 7 |
| Line 7: One word—noun, opposite of subject in line 1 |

Newspaper story headline: _____

Words that relate to your story:

_____

_____

_____

_____

## Diamante

1. _____

2. _____

3. _____

4. _____

5. _____

6. _____

7. _____

# Print Resources

Alber, S. R. 1999. "I don't like to write, but I love to get published": Using a classroom newspaper to motivate reluctant writers. *Reading & Writing Quarterly* 15 (4): 355–60.

Danielson, K. E., and S. E. Rogers. 2000. You can't pass it on if you don't have it: Encouraging lifelong reading. *Reading Horizons* 41 (1): 35–45.

Flippo, R. F. 2003. *Assessing readers: Qualitative diagnosis and instruction.* Portsmouth, NH: Heinemann.

Fry, E. B. 2004. *The vocabulary teacher's book of lists.* San Francisco: Jossey-Bass.

Fry, E. B., J. E. Kress, and D. L. Fountoukidis. 2000. *The reading teacher's book of lists.* 4th ed. San Francisco: Jossey-Bass.

Gardner, H. 1993. *Frames of mind: The theory of multiple intelligences.* New York: Basic.

———. 1993. *Multiple intelligences: The theory in practice.* New York: Basic.

———. 2000. *Intelligence reframed: Multiple intelligences for the 21st century.* New York: Basic.

Grimshaw, W. 2004. *Newspaper-based reading strategy instruction: Developing the fluency skills of third grade students as they "read all about it."* Fredericksburg, VA: Mary Washington College.

Hoyt, L. 2002. *Make it real: Strategies for success with informational texts.* Portsmouth, NH: Heinemann.

Kletzien, S., and M. Dreher. 2004. Using informational books for read-alouds. In *Informational Text in K–3 Classrooms,* 45–54. Newark, DE: International Reading Association.

Krajka, J. 2000. Some possibilities for using on-line newspapers in the ESL classroom. *Internet TESL Journal* 6 (4). Available at http://iteslj.org/Techniques/Krajka-OnlineNews.html.

Krashen, S. 2004. *The power of reading.* 2nd ed. Portsmouth, NH: Heinemann.

Meyer, M. 2002. *Measuring success! The positive impact of newspapers in education programs on student achievement.* Vienna, VA: Newspaper Association of America Foundation.

Olien, R. 2002. *Getting the most out of teaching with newspapers: Learning-rich lessons, strategies, and activities that use the power of newspapers to teach current events and build skills in reading, writing, math, and more.* New York: Scholastic.

Opitz, M. F., and M. P. Ford. 2001. *Reaching readers: Flexible & innovative strategies for guided reading.* Portsmouth, NH: Heinemann.

O'Reilly, J., and J. Alexander. 1998. Newspapers as a reading resource: Their impact on boys and on parental involvement. *Literacy* 32 (3): 21–26.

Rasinski, T. 2003. *The fluent reader.* New York: Scholastic.

Sanderson, P. 1999. *Using newspapers in the classroom.* Cambridge: Cambridge University Press.

Shaw, D. 2000. *Featuring the frameworks: Linking English/language arts to your newspaper.*

———. 2003. *Reading first: Research-based reading instruction using the newspaper.* Landover Hills, MD: Newspapers in Education Institute.

Sullivan, B. L., and P. Allen-Thompson. 1998. *The newspaper as an educative institution: Origins & rationale for using newspapers in education.* San Francisco: Use the News Foundation.

Tomlinson, C. A. 1999. *The differentiated classroom: Responding to the needs of all learners.* Alexandria, VA: Association for Supervision and Curriculum Development.

———. 2001. *How to differentiate instruction in mixed-ability classrooms.* 2nd ed. Alexandria, VA: Association for Supervision and Curriculum Development.

Tompkins, G. E. 2003. *50 literacy strategies: step by step.* Upper Saddle River, NJ: Prentice Hall.

Trelease, J. 2006. *The read-aloud handbook.* 6th ed. New York: Penguin.

# Web Sites for Newspapers

Make sure to visit the Newspapers in Education Web site (www. nieonline.com) to find free lessons by grade level and subject. The site also provides a database of other free resources offered by newspapers across America.

Many other newspaper resources are available online as well. Many newspapers offer their entire print editions for free online, and others provide a variety of free resources. If you use a particular newspaper frequently and that newspaper is not free, it may be in your best interest to become a subscriber. Always inquire about teacher and student discounts.

You can find the site for any newspaper by typing the name of that newspaper into an Internet search engine such as Google, MSN, AltaVista, or Yahoo! Following are the Web sites for the top twenty-five newspapers in the United States, based on daily print-edition circulation (as of 2006, courtesy of New York University's School of Journalism).

1. *USA Today:* www.usatoday.com
2. *The Wall Street Journal:* www.wsj.com
3. *The New York Times:* www.nytimes.com
4. *Los Angeles Times:* www.latimes.com
5. *The Washington Post:* www.washingtonpost.com
6. *New York Daily News:* www.nydailynews.com
7. *New York Post:* www.nypost.com
8. *Chicago Tribune:* www.chicagotribune.com
9. *Houston Chronicle:* www.chron.com
10. *The Dallas Morning News:* www.dallasnews.com
11. *San Francisco Chronicle:* www.sfgate.com/chronicle
12. *Newsday* (New York): www.newsday.com
13. *The Arizona Republic:* www.azcentral.com/arizonarepublic/
14. *Chicago Sun-Times:* www.suntimes.com
15. *The Boston Globe:* www.boston.com/news/globe
16. *The Atlanta Journal-Constitution:* www.ajc.com
17. *The Star-Ledger* (Newark, NJ): www.nj.com/starledger
18. *Star Tribune* (Minneapolis): www.startribune.com
19. *Detroit Free Press:* www.freep.com
20. *The Philadelphia Inquirer:* www.philly.com/inquirer
21. *The Plain Dealer* (Cleveland): www.cleveland.com/plaindealer
22. *St. Petersburg Times:* www.tampabay.com
23. *The Oregonian:* www.oregonlive.com/oregonian
24. *The San Diego Union-Tribune:* www.signonsandiego.com
25. *The Denver Post:* www.denverpost.com

# Other Useful Web Sites

Check out the following Web sites for additional information, as well as links to ideas for integrating differentiated instruction and multiple-intelligence strategies into your lessons.

www.businessballs.com/howardgardnermultipleintelligences.htm
www.cast.org/publications/ncac/ncac_diffinstruc.html
www.frsd.k12.nj.us/rfmslibrarylab/di/differentiated_instruction.htm
www.infed.org/thinkers/gardner.htm
www.internet4classrooms.com/di.htm
www.thomasarmstrong.com/multiple_intelligences.htm

# Index